# A GUIDE TO GETTING YOUR HOUSE IN ORDER

RONALD R. DOWLING
KAREN PRESCIA DOWLING

Printed in the United States of America

First Printing, 2017

Gradient Positioning Systems, LLC
4105 Lexington Avenue North, Suite 110
Arden Hills, MN 55126
(877) 901-0894

Contributors: Nick Stovall, Mike Binger, Nate Lucius and Gradient Positioning Systems, LLC.

# TABLE OF CONTENTS

**FOREWORD:** *IT'S A FAMILY AFFAIR*................................................1

**INTRODUCTION** ..............................................................3

**CHAPTER 1:** *THE PERKS OF LEGACY PLANNING* ......................13

**CHAPTER 2:** *PREPARING FOR RETIRED LIFE*.........................29

**CHAPTER 3:** *THE COLORS OF YOUR MONEY*..........................45

**CHAPTER 4:** *CREATING A LIFETIME OF INCOME* ...................57

**CHAPTER 5:** *WOMEN IN RETIREMENT* ..............................63

**CHAPTER 6:** *CREATING A SOCIAL SECURITY
MAXIMIZATION REPORT* ...........................73

**CHAPTER 7:** *HOW TO CREATE AN INCOME STREAM
WHILE PROTECTING YOUR PRINCIPAL*...................89

**CHAPTER 8:** *WAKE UP TO THE REALITIES: CATASTROPHIC
ILLNESS AND HOW TO PROTECT YOURSELF*.......109

**CHAPTER 9:** *ACCUMULATION*......................................125

**CHAPTER 10:** *THE POWER OF MANAGED MONEY* ..................135

**CHAPTER 11:** *NEW IDEAS FOR INVESTING* ........................151

**CHAPTER 12:** *TAXATION WITHOUT COMPLICATION*...............157

**CHAPTER 13:** *TAXES AND THE FUTURE* ............................169

**CHAPTER 14:** *THE BRANDEIS STORY* ..............................185

**CHAPTER 15:** *PREPARING YOUR LEGACY*...........................195

**CHAPTER 16:** *HOW TO CHOOSE A FINANCIAL
PROFESSIONAL* ..................................207

**GLOSSARY** ................................................................225

# FOREWORD
## IT'S A FAMILY AFFAIR

Retirement planning is simultaneously one of the most exciting and dreaded tasks that lay ahead of you. On one hand, you are taking action steps to create an enjoyable time of your life you have been looking forward to for decades. On the other, you have to wrestle with the collection of assets and liabilities you have and figure out how to begin providing yourself with a sustainable income that begins on the day you retire. It will need to last you for the rest of your life.

This kind of undertaking isn't one you have to go on alone. A good retirement plan is often the result of a good team of planners, including yourself. You may also need to get your family or loved ones involved. It is a family affair, largely because your family will play an important role in the way you organize some of your assets, who you choose as beneficiaries, how you structure your estate, and who you trust to assume responsibility of your estate in the event of your passing or a serious medical incident.

We believe the financial professionals you choose to work with should be like honorary family members. You need to trust them completely, communicate with them openly, and rely on them when you need to make difficult decisions. Working together with your family and your financial team, you can create a plan that anticipates your needs (both expected and unexpected), provides you with a lifetime of income, and passes on your estate efficiently and effectively in accordance with your wishes.

Before you enter into retirement, ask yourself this question: "What would I rate my retirement and estate plan on a scale of 1 to 10 right now?" How robust is it? How prepared are you for everything the future may throw at you? If you have doubts or questions, it is time to get answers before you run into those obstacles.

Today, the average retirement savings of a 50-year-old is $42,797. A fifty-year-old person can easily live another 30 or more years.* Without a plan, that money won't provide a lasting income, and those average 50-year-olds will have some difficult realities to face when they retire. Take the time to make a plan and secure your future for you and your family.

---

* statisticbrain.com http://www.statisticbrain.com/retirement-statistics/

# INTRODUCTION

Retirement always seems like a distant shore. It is something that will happen down the road. In the meantime, you're saving money, investing some, and counting on your 401(k) to finance your future. As a member of the workforce, you've been trained to save your money and accumulate your assets as you go. The goal, presumably, is retirement. You can save and contribute to your employer-sponsored retirement account without a plan. You just dedicate a certain percentage of your income and move on with your life. Retiring without a plan, however, isn't as easy.

During your working years, rate of return on your investments is paramount. You want your money to work for you, and you have dollar cost averaging on your side. You are regularly and consistently contributing to your savings and investments. As a retiree, it's time to shift your focus from returns to income and stability. This paradigm shift is a large one, and it may take some time to wrap your mind around it. Instead of earning more money, you now need to leverage your money to provide you with a lifetime of income.

This hasn't always been the case. Retirements of generations past have been funded by pensions, less volatile market investing, and other defined-benefit options. We are now entering a defined-contribution plan retirement landscape. Instead of retiring with a pension after working your whole life, we are now expected to rely on our own savings, investments, and retirement accounts: assets we are required to contribute to.

You can still relax and enjoy life as a retiree—it just might take more planning than you expected. Unlike the past, when a pension kicked in and you could depend on that income throughout retirement, you now have a portfolio of assets you need to organize in a way that will provide you with income, kind of like creating your own pension. Your portfolio might include a savings account, a 401(k), an IRA, market investments, real estate, or other assets.

Investing today, with market volatility at an all-time high and global economic conditions in flux, is more challenging than ever. Additionally, interest rates are at historic lows, taxes are projected to increase, and the cost of health care continues to rise. Are you prepared to create income for yourself and your spouse and to account for health care and legacy building?

You probably don't know, like many people. You might have enough money to retire, but retirement planning today is more than just having money. You need a plan that creates efficiency, crafted together with a financial professional.

## LEADING THE WAY

Retirement planning wasn't always a common concept. We may take for granted today that people have to plan to retire, but in the past many people could rely on a pension, Social Security benefits, and their market investments for income after they stopped working. It isn't always clear what kind of plan you need, how you make a plan, or what a plan is. Some people have consistently contributed to a 401(k) or IRA and they believe that is their plan. Some people are DIY investors and plan to keep playing the market to fund their retirement. Neither of those scenarios are true plans, however. Saving money and investing money are methods of accumulation. Retirement is about *distribution.*

The risk of running out of money in retirement is real. Life expectancies are increasing, health care costs are rising, and market volatility is hurting investors. We saw this first hand during the recession of 2008. Many people's savings were vulnerable when the market made a large correction. As a result, millions of people had to go back to work or delay retirement so they wouldn't run out of money.

You spent your career working for your money. Now it's time for your money to work for you and your family. Truly putting your money to work in an efficient and profitable plan requires more than investing in some good stocks or withdrawing from your IRA. A good plan is a comprehensive arrangement of all your assets, your liabilities, and your tax situation set against the backdrop of your goals for retirement, the costs you may face in the future, and your lifestyle. The goal is a durable, lifelong income that allows you to live the retired life you want. By creating and protecting a reliable stream of income, you create more freedom to leverage your other assets for growth, legacy building, travel, or other goals. When you know how much you need, you can begin to create a plan that works for *you.*

The chapters that follow outline an easy-to-follow methodology for organizing your assets, adjusting your portfolio to reflect your risk tolerance, creating a reliable stream of retirement income, and planning for taxes, health care costs, and legacy.

We are a husband and wife team with over 30 years of combined industry experience. During our tenure we have seen incredible success stories from proper planning, and financial travesties from a lack of it. Your retirement plan doesn't just affect you—it has an impact on your entire family. We pay attention to the details, recommend processes and plans over products, and act in your best interest always. If we wouldn't make a decision for us and our family, we wouldn't recommend it for you, either. That's our promise.

## MAKING SENSE OF YOUR FINANCES

Taking the time to organize your finances and plan your retirement might not be on your list of favorite pastimes. You'll be glad you took the time to do it, however, when you're enjoying a fully financed and stress-free retirement. Creating a plan requires some serious decision-making. Before you delve into those waters, it is important to reexamine the way you look at your money. When you were in the workforce, saving money for retirement, you regarded your money and assets in terms of their ability to grow. You prioritized growth, liquidity, and security in that order.

Income was a given, because you had a job and a steady paycheck. These accumulation years were the time you focused on rates of return, growth of your investments, and accumulating assets. Retirement is a different stage of your life, and it requires a different way of thinking about and using your money. Your focus now is not on the return from your investments, but the income you can draw from them. These are your distribution years, and your priorities surrounding money will be different. The order of your priorities shifts to security, income, growth, and liquidity. Notice how they are in a different order than during your accumulation years.

Security is your top priority during retirement. There are no more paychecks, there is no more overtime. Your working years are over and you are now responsible for your own income. You also don't have the same amount of time to earn money back after a market downturn or a big purchase. Your relationship with risk has changed dramatically, and your portfolio should reflect it.

## EIGHT HAZARDS TO YOUR NEST EGG

Saving money is the cornerstone of your retirement plan. You've been doing it your entire working life, and your savings and assets will help you create a plan to fund your retirement. Having money alone is not enough, however. Everything from inflation to bad advice can threaten your money and your retirement. These eight hazards to your nest egg can be avoided with awareness, careful planning, and sound advice:

1. **Running Out of Money.** One of the most common questions retirees have as they approach retirement is, "Do I have enough money to retire?" The question is a simple one, but the answer isn't. Discovering how much money you need requires accurate budgeting, asset organization, and an honest conversation about what your goals are for retirement. When you have an accurate budget and a full understanding of your assets, you can work with a professional and proprietary software to run projections on how long your money will last in different scenarios. You may need less money than you thought you did to create a secure stream of retirement income, giving you more freedom to travel or to leave less money in the stock market. Alternatively, you may need to tighten up ship, so to speak, and preserve as much of your savings as you can to achieve that income. Whatever your situation is, once you know what you need to do to secure your retirement income, you can follow your plan and have peace of mind.

2. **Bad Information.** Everybody and their brother-in-law has advice about how to invest. Free advice isn't always good advice, however. Professional advice isn't always given in your best interest either, for that matter. Unless someone knows the details of your financial situation, understands your personal goals for retirement, and is bound and motivated to act in your best interest, it is almost impossible for them to give you helpful guidance. Celebrity investors and brokers recommend specific financial products and strategies all the time. That kind of advice isn't designed for *you*. No single product or solution can work for everyone. Discovering what is right for you is the backbone of the retirement planning process.

3. **The Real Risk of Inflation.** Inflation may seem like a benign reality of the financial world, but if unplanned for it can pose a serious risk to the stability of your retirement. The consumer price index reports that the average rate of inflation from 1994 to 2014 was over 2 percent. * If you left your money in the bank, you would actually have lost money over the time period—not because of market volatility or recessions—because of inflation. Hedging against inflation needs to be part of your retirement plan. Leveraging your assets to secure your income can free up your remaining money to be used for growth.

4. **Health Care Costs.** Long-term care is an increasing reality for aging Americans. Seventy percent of people turning 65 years old today will need long-term care, as reported by the U.S. Department of Health and Human Services. Many people are unprepared for this hazard to their nest egg. Nursing care can costs hundreds of dollars per day. It

---

* *Consumer Price Index, December 31, 1994 through December 31, 2014.*

is vital to protect your assets specifically against this risk. There are many options available to you, many of which are discussed in Chapter 8.

5. **Market Volatility.** You know market volatility poses risks for investors, but the extent of that risk may be greater than you think. The 2017 DALBAR study provides some helpful insight. According to the study, average investors suffer from market volatility in unique ways because of emotional investing. Emotional investing often prevents people from remaining invested for long enough periods to reap benefits, and causes people to buy and sell haphazardly. Instead of investing with a strategy, many investors react to the market and end up losing out. Instead of riding the market rollercoaster with your retirement income on the line, you can benefit by creating a secure line of income from protected assets before you venture into the market.

6. **Tax Burdens.** You paid taxes during your working years, and you'll pay taxes while retired. Planning for this can help save you thousands in the long run. Not planning for it can cost you dearly. You may underestimate how large of an impact inefficient tax planning can have on your future. Creating tax-advantaged and tax-efficient assets and strategies before you retire can help you prepare for a retirement with a lower tax price tag. The same goes for legacy planning. There are many strategies and tools that can help you create a tax-free or tax-advantaged legacy for your loved ones.

7. **Loss of Income from Death or Divorce:** When faced with losing a spouse through either death or divorce, there is approximately a 40 percent reduction of income due to lost pensions or disability and/or lower Social Security

benefits. Having a plan to replace that income in the case of an untimely loss can substantially improve your financial position. Chapter 5 addresses how these issues impact women, since most women will outlive their spouses by six to eight years and may be faced with this situation.

8. **Bad Legacy Planning.** Planning the distribution and management of your legacy can give you peace of mind, save your loved ones a lot of money, and eliminate potential conflicts. Think about what you want your legacy to look like and what goals you have, then work with a professional to structure your assets to achieve those goals. File the paperwork, have the conversations, and organize your assets before you pass away so your wishes will be followed. Planning your legacy properly can also give you and your loved ones more privacy by keeping your assets out of the public probate process.

## WORK WITH SOMEONE YOU TRUST

Retirement is a huge achievement. All the time you have worked and all the money you have saved have led you to this point. The money and assets you have accumulated represent so much more than numbers on a printout or a computer screen. Instead of drifting into retirement hoping you'll have enough money, you owe it to yourself and your family to put careful thought and planning into how you leverage that money and those assets. Find and work with someone you trust who has your best interests at heart before you make the big decisions that will impact the rest of your financial future.

Dowling Consulting Services, Inc. brings experience, intention, and fiduciary responsibility to the table for each and every client we meet with. We aren't selling anything. We are working together with people to create successful retirement plans. Our team consists of independent attorneys, experienced CPAs, insurance specialists, and money managers so we make sure every detail is addressed and every possibility is considered.

Your money is important, but your plan is the true power of your retirement. Money and assets won't organize themselves in the efficient and effective ways you need for a lasting retirement plan. Your plan will be unique to you and should reflect your desires and your particular way of approaching life. You'll never regret making a thorough, specialized financial methodology for your retirement savings.

All our best,

Ron Dowling, *Strategic Consultant at Dowling Consulting Services, Inc.*
Karen Dowling, *CEO/President of Dowling Consulting Services, Inc.*

## ABOUT KAREN

Karen P. Dowling holds an Accounting degree and an MBA. Her work in the financial management field has included accounting, professional and business consulting and life coaching. Karen currently holds a Series 65 license and she is an investment advisor representative for Chancellor Financial Services, Inc. Karen's mission is to assist clients in planning for the retirement they have always dreamed of, one that will provide them peace of mind & financial freedom throughout their lifetime.

## ABOUT RON

Ronald R. Dowling has been in the financial services industry for more than 30 years. He has focused on legacy planning, Medicaid strategies and retirement planning. He is a Certified Estate Planner (CEP) and a Certified Elder Care Specialist. He has dedicated his career to helping people put their affairs in order and leave a legacy for their heirs.

# 1

# THE PERKS OF LEGACY PLANNING

If you're like most people, planning your estate isn't on the top of your list of favorite things to do. Taking the time to make a plan, however, can have a huge impact on your loved ones and on your legacy. Consider the story of Pablo Picasso, the famous artist. In 1973, at the age of 91, Picasso died and left behind a massive fortune in assets. His estate included over 45,000 pieces of original artwork, five homes, and large amounts of cash, gold and bonds. He died intestate, leaving no will. It took more than six years to settle his estate at a cost of over $30 million. The battle is still being waged, however, as his artwork continues to generate revenue.

Not all of us are billionaire artists, but we all leave things behind. Stating your intentions and making a plan for the distribution of your estate can help you preserve the value of your legacy and help it have the kind of lasting effect you intend it to.

Planning your income needs for retirement, managing your assets and just living your life without worrying about how your estate will be handled when you are gone make legacy planning less than attractive for a Saturday afternoon task. **The fact of the matter, however, is that if you don't plan your legacy, someone else will.** That someone else is usually a combination of the IRS and other government entities: lawyers, executors, courts, and accountants. Who do you think has the best interests of your beneficiaries in mind?

## EVERYONE MAKES MISTAKES

Picasso isn't the only famous person to have made the mistake of not properly planning their estate. These high profile stories can act as cautionary tales, reminding us that even a little planning can go a long way. We all make mistakes, but hopefully you won't make the mistake of not planning your legacy. When your money and the future of your loved ones are on the line, estate planning can have large, personal impacts.

Your legacy and your loved ones shouldn't suffer the penalties of unnecessary taxes, court costs, and attorney fees. Organizing your estate planning documents, including trusts, wills, power of attorney and beneficiary designations, will ensure that the assets you worked so hard to accumulate and maintain will continue to benefit the people you love after you are gone.

Because this is such an important part of estate planning, you should make sure you are working with someone who is qualified and experienced, and who is legally bound to act in your best interest. You want to be confident that the "I"s are dotted and the "T's" are crossed and that everything is correct. An experienced professional can also point out inefficiencies in your plan, loopholes you might take advantage of, and help you sidestep unnecessary expenses. A professional who cares about your plan will also take the time to meet with you regularly to update your documents and adjust your plan to account for any changes in your life.

## TAKING CONTROL OF YOUR LEGACY

A legacy is more than the sum total of the financial assets you have accumulated. It is the lasting impression you make on those you leave behind. The dollars and cents are just a small part of a legacy.

A legacy encompasses the stories that others tell about you, shared experiences and values. An estate may pay for college tuition, but a legacy may inform your grandchildren about the importance of higher education and self-reliance.

A legacy may also contain family heirlooms or items of emotional significance. It may be a piece of art your great-grandmother painted, family photos, or a childhood keepsake.

When you go about planning your legacy, certainly explore strategies that can maximize the financial benefit to the ones you care about. But also take the time to ensure that you have organized the whole of your legacy, and let that be a part of the last gift you leave.

Many people avoid planning their legacy until they feel they must. Something may change in your life, like the birth of a grandchild, the diagnosis of a serious health problem, or the death of a close friend or loved one. Waiting for tragedy to strike in order to get your affairs in order is not the best course of action. The emotional stress of that kind of situation can make it hard to make patient, thoughtful decisions. Taking the time to create a premeditated and thoughtful legacy plan will assure that your assets will be transferred where and when you want them when the time comes.

## THE BENEFITS OF PLANNING YOUR LEGACY

The distribution of your assets, whether in the form of property, stocks, Individual Retirement Accounts, 401(k)s or liquid assets, can be a complicated undertaking if you haven't left clear instructions about how you want them handled. Not having a plan will cost more money and take more time, leaving your loved ones to wait (sometimes for years) and receive less of your legacy than if you had a clear plan.

Planning your legacy will help your assets be transferred with little delay and little confusion. Instead of leaving decisions about how to distribute your estate to your family, attorneys or financial professionals, preserve your legacy and your wishes by drafting a clear plan at an early age.

And while you know all that, it can still be hard to sit down and do it. It reminds you that life is short, and the relatively complicated nature of sorting through your assets can feel like a daunting task. But one thing is for sure: ***it is impossible for your assets to be transferred or distributed the way you want at the end of your life if you don't have a plan.***

Ask yourself:

- Are my assets up to date?
- Have my primary and contingent beneficiaries been clearly designated?
- Does my plan allow for restriction of a beneficiary?
- Does my legacy plan address minor children that I want to provide with income?
- Does my legacy plan allow for multi-generational payout?

Answers to these questions are critical if you want the final say in how your assets are distributed. In order to achieve your legacy goals, you need a plan.

## MAKING A PLAN

Eventually, when your income need is filled and you have sufficient standby money to meet your need for emergencies, travel or other extra expenses you are planning for, whatever isn't used during your lifetime becomes your financial legacy. The money that you do not use during your lifetime will either go to loved ones, unloved ones, charity, or the IRS. The question is, who would you rather disinherit?

By having a legacy plan that clearly outlines your assets, your beneficiaries and your distribution goals, you can make sure that your money and property is ending up in the hands of the people you determine beforehand. Is it really that big of a deal? It absolutely is. Think about it. Without a clear plan, it is impossible for anyone to know if your beneficiary designations are current and reflect your wishes because you haven't clearly expressed who your beneficiaries are. You may have an idea of who you want your assets to go to, but without a plan, it is anyone's guess. It is also impossible to know if the titling of your assets is accurate unless you have gone through and determined whose name is on the titles. More importantly, *if you have not clearly and effectively communicated your desires regarding the planned distribution of your legacy, you and your family may end up losing a large part of it.*

As you can see, managing a legacy is more complicated than having an attorney read your will, divide your estate and write checks to your heirs. The additional issue of taxes, Family Maximum Benefit calculations and a host of other decisions rear their heads. Educating yourself about the best options for positioning your legacy assets is a challenging undertaking. Working with a financial professional who is versed in determining the most efficient and effective ways of preserving and distributing your legacy can save you time, money and strife.

So, how do you begin?

**Making a Legacy Plan Starts with a Simple List.** The first, and one of the largest, steps to setting up an estate plan with a financial professional that reflects your desires is creating a detailed inventory of your assets and debts (if you have any). You need to know what assets you have, who the beneficiaries are, how much they are worth and how they are titled. You can start by identifying and listing your assets. This is a good starting point for working with a financial professional who can then help you determine the detailed information about your assets that will dictate how they are distributed upon your death.

If you are particularly concerned about leaving your kids and grandkids a lifetime of income with minimal taxes, you will want to discuss a Stretch IRA option with your financial professional.

## STRETCH IRAS: GETTING THE MOST OUT OF YOUR MONEY

In 1986, the U.S. Congress passed a law that allows for multi-generational distributions of IRA assets. This type of distribution is called a Stretch IRA because it stretches the distribution of the account out over a longer period of time to several beneficiaries. It also allows the account to continue accumulating value throughout your relatives' lifetimes. You can use a Stretch IRA as an income tool that distributes throughout your lifetime, your children's lifetimes and your grandchildren's lifetimes.

Stretch IRAs are an attractive option for those more concerned with creating income for their loved ones than leaving them with a lump sum that may be subject to a high tax rate. With traditional IRA distributions, non-spousal beneficiaries must generally take distributions from their inherited IRAs, whether transferred or not, within five years after the death of the IRA owner. An exception to this rule applies if the beneficiary elects to take distributions over his or her lifetime, which is referred to as stretching the IRA.

## Beneficiaries Stretch IRA Distributions

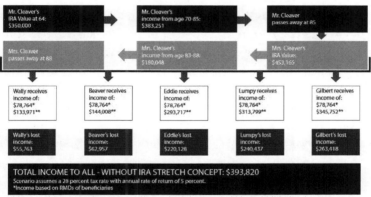

| | | |
|---|---|---|
| Mr. Cleaver's IRA Value at 64: $350,000 | Mr. Cleaver's income from age 70-85: $383,251 | Mr. Cleaver passes away at 85 |
| Mrs. Cleaver passes away at 88 | Mrs. Cleaver's income from age 83-88: $180,048 | Mrs. Cleaver's IRA Value: $453,165 |

| Wally receives income of: $133,971* | Beaver receives income of: $144,008* | Eddie receives income of: $293,717* | Lumpy receives income of: $313,799* | Gilbert receives income of: $345,752* |
|---|---|---|---|---|

**TOTAL INCOME TO ALL - IRA STRETCH CONCEPT: $1,231,248**
Scenario assumes a 28 percent tax rate with annual rate of return of 5 percent
*Income based on RMDs of beneficiaries

## Beneficiaries FAIL to Stretch IRA Distributions

| | | |
|---|---|---|
| Mr. Cleaver's IRA Value at 64: $350,000 | Mr. Cleaver's income from age 70-85: $383,251 | Mr. Cleaver passes away at 85 |
| Mrs. Cleaver passes away at 88 | Mrs. Cleaver's income from age 83-88: $180,048 | Mrs. Cleaver's IRA Value: $453,165 |

| Wally receives income of: $78,764* $133,971** | Beaver receives income of: $78,764* $144,008** | Eddie receives income of: $78,764* $293,717** | Lumpy receives income of: $78,764* $313,799** | Gilbert receives income of: $78,764* $345,752** |
|---|---|---|---|---|
| Wally's lost income: $55,763 | Beaver's lost income: $62,957 | Eddie's lost income: $220,128 | Lumpy's lost income: $240,437 | Gilbert's lost income: $263,418 |

**TOTAL INCOME TO ALL - WITHOUT IRA STRETCH CONCEPT: $393,820**
Scenario assumes a 28 percent tax rate with annual rate of return of 5 percent.
*Income based on RMDs of beneficiaries

\* Lump sum after tax income upon death of Mrs. Cleaver.   \*\* Lifetime income based on RMD of beneficiary - see above.

Let's begin by looking at the potential of stretching an IRA throughout multiple generations.

As the illustrations with the Cleaver family show, stretching an IRA over multiple generations can have a large impact on the total amount of income that it is able to provide. In the top illustration, Mr. Cleaver's IRA is stretched so it provides his children with multiple distributions throughout their lifetimes. By the time the account is empty, Mr. Cleaver's $350,000 IRA has been turned into a legacy of more than $1.2 million for the entire Cleaver family. But look at what happens when the IRA is not stretched: after Mr. and Mrs. Cleaver pass away, the IRA is divided between the five children and distributed to each as a single lump sum. In that scenario, the IRA only provides the Cleaver family with a total income of $393,820. For the Cleavers, not choosing to stretch the IRA would cost them nearly $800,000 in lost income.

Unfortunately, many things may also play a role in failing to stretch IRA distributions. It can be tempting for a beneficiary to take a lump sum of money despite the tax consequences. Fortunately, if you want to solidify your plan for distribution, there are options that will allow you to open up an IRA and incorporate "spendthrift" clauses for your beneficiaries. This will ensure your legacy is stretched appropriately and to your specifications. Only certain insurance companies allow this option, and you will not find this benefit with any brokerage accounts. You need to work with a financial professional who has the appropriate relationship with an insurance company that provides this option.

> *Chester organized his assets long ago. He started planning his retirement early and made investment decisions that would meet his needs. He was able to fill his income gap (the difference between the amount of money you can depend on for income each month and the amount you need to maintain your lifestyle and meet your expenses) by positioning investments to create income while protecting his principal, and by a well-planned managed money strategy overseen by his financial professional. This allowed him to focus on ways to grow and maximize his wealth throughout his retirement. He reorganized his Know So and Hope So Money (as we will discuss in Chapter 3) as he got older, making sure to*

*balance his assets along the way so they continued to provide him with the income he needed without exposing his portfolio to increased market risk.*

*He also maximized his Social Security benefit. When Chester retired, he had created an income plan that allowed him to continue accumulating wealth during his retirement. At this point, he turned his attention to planning his legacy. His goal was to pass his estate to his son and daughter as efficiently as possible, and without probate costs. He was aware of financial horror stories involving court fees and state-directed asset distribution. He wanted to avoid probate all together, but didn't know how.*

*Chester met with an attorney to draw up a will, but he quickly learned that while having a will was a good plan, it wasn't the most efficient way to distribute his estate. In fact, relying solely on a will would create several roadblocks. Avoiding probate and the unintentional disinheritance of his children, he would have to learn more about big picture estate planning with someone who knew the ropes.*

## UNDERSTANDING THE ELEMENTS OF YOUR LEGACY: WILLS, POWER OF ATTORNEY AND LIVING TRUSTS

When most people think about an estate, it may seem like something only the very wealthy have: a stately manor or an enormous business. No matter who you are or what you own, you have an estate of some kind. Big or small, your estate consists of every asset you have earned and maintained over your lifetime. You may think of assets as investments, but there is a much broader spectrum to consider. Assets include real estate, savings, stocks, bonds, life insurance policies, possessions, heirlooms, business interests, and retirement plans. It would be heartbreaking to have the things that represent your work and your life mismanaged or eroded by fees and legal costs. Doing some planning ahead of time can help you protect your assets and your legacy. Remember Picasso? As wealthy as he was, his heirs lost millions simply because he didn't have a plan!

## THE POWER AND LIMITATIONS OF A WILL

The most expensive legacy plan is no plan at all. Without a plan or a will, like Picasso, the state has the authority to distribute your estate. This can include all of your assets and guardianship for minor children. The entire process is also public, and does not protect your privacy or the privacy of your loved ones.

A will is a good start to legacy planning, and can protect you in several ways. Most notably, a will can establish guardianship over your children if you pass away. The probate process is often still mandatory even when a will is in place. Structuring your IRA to pass to your beneficiaries can protect that asset, but your other assets may still be subject to probate. Additionally, if your estate is entirely distributed via your will, the money that your family may need to cover the costs of your medical bills, funeral expenses and estate taxes will be tied up in probate, which can last up to a year or more. While immediate family members may have the option of requesting immediate cash from your assets during probate to cover immediate health care expenses, taxes, and fees, that process comes with its own set of complications. Choosing alternative methods for distributing your legacy can make life easier for your loved ones and can help them claim more of your estate in a more timely fashion than traditional methods.

## UNDERSTANDING PROBATE

A will, while better than no legacy plan at all, exposes you to several weaknesses:
- Court involvement / legal fees
- The unintentional disinheritance of your beneficiaries
- Expenses related to the probate process

Having a will as a legacy plan can trigger probate. Put simply, probate is court oversight of your asset distribution. Unless you have made a clear legacy plan and discussed options for avoiding probate, it is highly likely that you have many assets that might pass through probate needlessly. *If your will and beneficiary designations aren't correctly structured, some of these assets will go through the probate process, which can turn dollars into cents.*

If you have a will, probate is usually just a formality. There is little risk that your will won't be executed per your instructions. The problem arises when the costs and lengthy timeline that probate creates come into play. Probate proceedings are notoriously expensive, lengthy and ponderous. A typical probate process identifies all of your assets and debts, pays any taxes and fees that you owe (including estate tax), pays court fees, and distributes your property and assets to your heirs. This process usually takes at least a year, and can take even longer before your heirs actually receive anything that you have left for them. For this reason, and because of the sometimes exorbitant fees that may be charged by lawyers and accountants during the process, probate has earned a nasty reputation.

The good news is these problems can be avoided with some planning. There are other important documents you can prepare and rely on to protect your privacy, your asset distribution, and your legacy. These documents include:

- Health POAs
- HIPAA Form
- Financial Power of Attorney
- Living or Pour-over Will
- and a Living Trust

## THE BENEFITS OF FINANCIAL POWER OF ATTORNEY

Aging can present mental and physical challenges to your health. If your health is affected by a stroke, chronic illness, or mentally disabling condition, the courts may decide to put someone else in charge of your financial management and decision making. They can do this even if you have a will. Their involvement will likely span the length of your illness or condition, or until you die. The courts can also take decision making power away from your family and control when and how your assets and estate are distributed. This probably isn't the way you want your legacy to be handled. You can avoid this scenario by establishing Financial Power of Attorney

The Financial Power of Attorney designation gives you the power to appoint someone to make financial decisions for you if you aren't able. It can save you and your family thousands of dollars in court and legal fees. It also gives you control of your legacy and finances by giving decision making power to someone you trust. You can also determine the specific responsibilities of your appointed decision maker.

## THE LIVING TRUST

A Living Trust is another key element to a secure legacy plan. This legal document creates a trust that you control. You can transfer ownership of your assets to the trust. They remain in your control and the trust protects them from probate in some key ways. Assets protected by a living trust can include vehicles, real estate, investments, etc. Creating a Financial Power of Attorney can give your proxy control of the trust, and all of the assets in it, protecting them from the courts and from probate.

A Living Trust helps you avoid probate altogether by structuring your legacy to be distributed outside of the probate process. Two other ways of doing this are by structuring your assets inside a life insurance plan, and by using individual retirement planning tools like IRAs that give you the option of designating a beneficiary upon your death.

One large and important difference between a living trust and a will is that a living trust goes into effect immediately, keeping you in control of your assets and giving your proxy control of them if you die or become incapacitated.

Your living trust allows you to control the timing of the distribution of your assets, as well. It can also benefit you in the following ways:

- By protecting special-needs dependents
- Securing income for your beneficiaries
- Reducing or eliminating estate taxes and fees
- Avoiding probate and the costs and delays associated with it
- Peace of mind

You can create a living trust at any time and start taking advantage of its benefits. It is a relatively inexpensive precaution you can take that can help you control your legacy, its distribution, and the taxes and fees it is subject to.

## PROTECT YOUR FAMILY BY PLANNING YOUR LEGACY

You would never want to unintentionally disinherit a loved one or loved ones because of confusion surrounding your legacy plan. Unfortunately, it happens. Why? This terrible situation is typically caused by a simple lack of understanding. In particular, mistakes regarding legacy distribution occur with regard to those whom people care for the most: their grandchildren.

One of the most important ways to plan for the inheritance of your grandchildren is by properly structuring the distribution of your legacy. Specifically, you need to know if your legacy is going to be distributed *per stirpes* or *per capita*.

**Per Stirpes.** *Per stirpes* is a legal term in Latin that means "by the branch." Your estate will be distributed *per stirpes* if you designate each branch of your family to receive an equal share of your estate. In the event that your children predecease you, their share will be distributed evenly between their children—your grandchildren.

**Per Capita.** *Per capita* distribution is different in that you may designate different amounts of your estate to be distributed to members of the same generation.

Per stirpes distribution of assets will follow the family tree down the line as the predecessor beneficiaries pass away. On the other hand, per capita distribution of assets ends on the branch of the family tree with the death of a designated beneficiary. For example, when your child passes away, in a per capita distribution, your grandchildren would not receive distributions from the assets that you designated to your child.

What the terms mean is not nearly as important as what they do, however. The reality is that improperly titled assets could accidentally leave your grandchildren disinherited upon the death of their parents. It's easy to check, and it's even easier to fix.

A simple way to remember the difference between the two types of distribution goes something like this: "***Stirpes are forever and Capita is capped.***"

Another way to avoid complicated legacy distribution problems, and the probate process, is by leveraging a life insurance plan.

## CHAPTER 1 RECAP //

- Proper legacy planning is important, no matter your net worth. Failing to do so can cost your loved ones thousands of dollars.
- A qualified financial professional can help you structure your legacy plan to protect your wishes, your beneficiaries, and your assets.
- Creating a Stretch IRA, or Beneficiary IRA, can help you provide income for you, your spouse, and your beneficiaries. A Stretch IRA can be distributed in smaller payouts over the course of a beneficiary's lifetime. This lets them enjoy a regular income stream, and gives them the benefit of compounding interest over time.
- Legacy planning begins with a simple list.
- A will provides your legacy with some protection, but it does not eliminate the probate process. States individually determine when an estate qualifies for probate. It is important to maintain current and accurate beneficiary designations on your assets to protect them.
- Probate is the court-directed distribution of your estate. The court identifies all of your assets and debts, pays any taxes and fees that you owe (including estate tax), pays court fees, and distributes your property and assets to your heirs. This process usually takes at least a year, and it can take even longer before your heirs actually receive anything that you have left for them. The costs of this process are charged to your estate.
- Establishing a Financial Power of Attorney and creating a living trust can help you avoid the delays and expenses of the probate process. This type of planning can also help you have more control over how and when your legacy is distributed. You also have control over who is in charge of your assets and their distribution.

# 2

# PREPARING FOR RETIRED LIFE

*Stay healthy, active, and happy after you retire.*

Planning for income and preparing your legacy are critical first steps when creating your retirement plan. Your assets and your need for income are defining variables in your retirement puzzle. Protecting your assets so they can work for you as long as you live and contribute to your legacy, and generating income that will last the rest of your life are on top of the retirement planning To-Do list.

Once you have met those needs, however, you enter a stage of retirement planning with less defined steps. Retired life is different than any other stage of life you have lived. Joys, challenges, new opportunities, and an entirely different set of needs will surface. It can be helpful to start thinking about what you want your retirement to look and feel like before you enter it so you can prepare yourself for a happy and successful retired life.

Retirement planning isn't just about the money. What will make you happy during retirement? What are some of your goals? What are things you've always wanted to do and put off until you were retired? Thinking about the answers to these questions may influence how to structure your assets, your income, and your legacy.

> » *Will your Social Security benefit, savings and other retirement assets be enough? If you're like Becky and Jim, you hope so. When the couple turned 60 years old, they started thinking about what their lives would be like in the next 10 years. When would they retire? What would their retirement look like? How much money did they have?*
>
> *They could both count on Social Security benefits, but neither one really knew how much their monthly checks would be, or when to file for them. Jim had a modest pension that he could begin collecting at age 67. He had always hoped to retire before that age. Becky had a 401(k), but she honestly wasn't exactly sure how it worked, how she could draw money from it and how much income it would provide once she retired.*

While Becky and Jim may sound like they're totally in the dark about their retirement, the truth is there are a lot of people just like them. They know retirement is coming and know they have some assets to rely on, but they aren't sure how it will all come together to provide them with a retirement income.

You spend your entire working life hoping what you put into your retirement accounts will help you live comfortably once you clock out of the workforce for good. The key word in that sentiment and the word that can make retirement feel like a looming problem instead of a rewarding life stage, is *hope*. You hope you'll have enough money.

Leaving your retirement up to chance is unadvisable by nearly any standard, yet millions of people find themselves *hoping* instead of planning for a happy ending. With information, tools and professional guidance, creating a successful retirement plan can put you in control of your financial management. From a purely financial perspective, the primary challenge of planning for a long, secure retirement is preparing for the day your paycheck stops and you need to turn a lifetime of savings into an income you cannot outlive. It is something quite unlike any financial challenge you have faced before.

Retirement is more than kicking back and cashing in on your Social Security benefit. Not only are there thousands of different options for each individual that affect when and how to file for Social Security benefits, there are thousands more for how to structure other assets like individual retirement accounts (IRAs), 401(k)s, life insurance policies, and investment portfolios. Each person's retirement is as unique as they are. Discovering the most efficient and effective way to leverage your assets for a comfortable retirement starts with an understanding of your goals and opportunities. You can discover these through a conversation with your financial professional, with your spouse, and with yourself.

## TAKING ADVANTAGE OF YOUR RETIREMENT

You need money to retire, but it doesn't end there. It is important to financially prepare for retirement, but retirement isn't all about the numbers. When you think about your retired life, you probably imagine your monthly income, your asset growth, or monthly index reports. You probably think about how you will spend your time, who you will spend it with, and what you will enjoy after leaving the workforce.

Planning for what you want to do will help you secure a high quality of life. You can't buy a financial product that will guarantee you happiness and fulfillment. You can have conversations with a financial professional who has your best interests at heart and who will help you plan the retirement you truly want. You might even think of the non-financial aspects of your retirement as the true foundation of your plan. The money comes in later to help you achieve your goals.

Asking yourself questions about your retirement can help you clarify what you want and what you don't. Retirement will be different than the rest of your life, so start by asking yourself the following questions:

- What things do you like to do? How do you like to spend your time? Do you like being productive, traveling, relaxing, etc.?
- What is your plan for staying healthy, engaged, and active? It is important to have purpose to maintain your health.
- Do you like to maintain robust social interactions? If so, how do you plan on staying engaged in your community? How will you meet new people?

The desires to learn, travel, invest, volunteer, etc. all need to be built into your retirement plan, just like your plan for income and asset protection.

In addition to hopes and goals, it is also common to have concerns and fears about retirement. Planning your retirement ahead of time allows you to face your fears head on and find solutions before problems ever arise. You can also use your retirement planning process to highlight the specific uses and goals you have for the money you have saved. You may want to designate some cash or investments for a grandchild's education, a large purchase, or a business venture. Creating a big picture plan that includes all of your intentions will help you achieve your goals and confront your fears.

The following set of questions can help you start identifying your goals and concerns for retirement:

- Do you have a plan to make sure you won't outlive your money? Do you feel like you have sufficient assets to fund your retirement?
- Do you want to shield your portfolio from market volatility?
- Are you aware of how taxes fit into your retirement plan and how they will affect you?
- What kind of legacy do you want to leave? How do you want to leave it?
- Do you want to plan for unexpected healthcare costs, including long-term illness or emergency medical expenses?

Facing your fears, preparing your legacy to protect your estate, and organizing your assets to provide you with income and protection will set you up for success and give you incredible peace of mind.

Making sure your assets last for your lifetime will depend on how you decide to invest them, and in what order you will spend them. With forces like inflation, market volatility, and fluctuating interest rates working against you, knowing what to do with your assets has never been more important. And the difference between making a good decision and a bad decision has never had such a dramatic impact on how people retire.

## 21ST CENTURY RETIREMENT

Advice about what to do with money has been around as long as money has existed. Hindsight allows us to see which advice was good and which advice didn't cut the mustard. Some sources of advice have been around for a very long time. While there are some basic investment concepts that have stood the test of time, most strategies that work adapt to changing conditions in the market, in the economy and the world, as well as changes in your personal circumstances.

The reality is that investment strategies and savings plans that worked in the past have encountered challenging new circumstances that have turned them on their heads. The Great Recession of the early 2000's highlighted how old investment ideas were not only ineffective but incredibly destructive to the retirement plans of millions of Americans. The dawn of an entirely restructured health care system brings with it new options and challenges that will undoubtedly change the way insurance companies provide investment products and services.

Perhaps the most important lessons investors learned from the Great Recession is that not understanding where your money is invested (and the potential risks of those investments) can work against you, your plans for retirement and your legacy. Saving and investing money isn't enough to truly get the most out of it. You must have a planful approach to managing your assets. Advice from someone you can trust can make a huge difference in the way you manage your 401(k) account(s). When you retire, you don't have the luxury of being able to wait until markets are moving up to withdraw from your accounts for income. You can't rely on markets to behave the way you need them to when you need them to. That is why it is important to create a plan that removes some of your assets from that risk so you can form a bedrock of dependable income.

Essentially, managing your money and your investments is an ongoing process that requires customization and adaptation to a changing world. And make no mistake; the world is always changing. What worked for your parents or even your parents' parents was probably good advice back then. People in retirement or approaching retirement today need new ideas and professional guidance.

## HOPE SO VS. KNOW SO MONEY

Let's take a look at some of the basic truths about money as it relates to saving for retirement. There are essentially two kinds of money: *Hope So* and *Know So*. Everyone can divide their money into these two categories. Some have more of one kind than the other. The goal isn't to eliminate one kind of money but to balance them as you approach retirement.

Hope So Money is money that is at risk. It fluctuates with the market. It has no minimum guarantee. It is subject to investor activity, stock prices, market trends, buying trends, etc. You get the picture. This money is exposed to more risk but also has the potential for more reward. Because the market is subject to change, you can't really be sure what the value of your investments

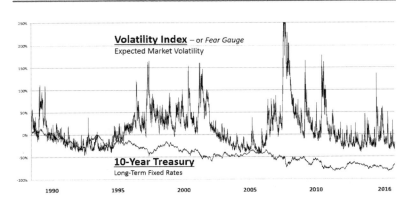

*The VIX, or volatility index, of the market represents expected market volatility. When the VIX Drops, economic experts expect less volatility. When the VIX rises, more volatility is expected.*

1. *VIX is a trademarked ticker symbol for the Chicago Board Options Exchange (CBOE) Market Volatility Index, a popular measure of the implied volatility of S&P 500 index options. Often referred to as the fear index or the fear gauge, it represents one measure of the market's expectation of stock market volatility over the next 30 day period. (wikipedia.com)*

2. *The CBOE 10-Year Treasury note (TNX) is based on 10 times the yield-to-maturity on the most recently auctioned 10-year Treasury note.*

will be worth in the future. You can't really *rely* on it at all. For this reason, we refer to it as Hope So Money. This doesn't mean you shouldn't have some money invested in the market, but it would be dangerous to assume you can know what it will be worth in the future.

Hope So Money is an important element of a retirement plan, especially in the early stages of planning when you can trade volatility for potential returns, and when a longer investment timeframe is available to you. In the long run, time can smooth out the ups and downs of money exposed to the market. Working with a professional and leveraging a long-term investment strategy has the potential to create rewarding returns from Hope So Money.

Know So Money, on the other hand, is safer when compared to Hope So Money. Know So Money is made up of dependable, low-risk or no-risk money, and investments that you can count on. Social Security is one of the most common forms of Know So Money. Income you draw or will draw from Social Security is guaranteed. You have paid into Social Security your entire career, and you can rely on that money during your retirement. Unlike the market, rates of growth for Know So Money are dependent on 10-year treasury rates. The 10-year treasury, or TNX, is commonly considered to represent a very secure and safe place for your money, hence Know So Money. The 10-year treasury drives key rates for things such as mortgages or CDs. Know So Money may not be as exciting as Hope So Money, but it is safer. You can safely be fairly sure you will have it in the future.

Knowing the difference between Hope So and Know So Money is an important step towards a successful retirement plan. People who are 55 or older and who are looking ahead to retirement should be relying on more Know So Money than Hope So Money.

Ideally, the rates of return on Hope So and Know So Money would have an overlapping area that provided an acceptable rate of risk for both types of money. In the early 1990s, interest rates were high and market volatility was low. At that time, you could invest in either Hope So or Know So Money options because the rates of return were similar from both Know So and Hope So investments, and you were likely to be fairly successful with a wide range of investment options. At that time, you could expose yourself to an acceptable amount of risk or an acceptable fixed rate. Basically, it was difficult to make a mistake during that time period. Today, you don't have those options. Market volatility is at all-time highs while interest rates are at all-time lows. They are so far apart from each other that it is hard to know what to do with your money.

Yesterday's investment rules may not work today. Not only could they hamper achieving your goals, they may actually harm your financial situation. We are currently in a period when the rates for Know So Money options are at historic lows, and the volatility of Hope So Money is higher than ever. There is no overlapping acceptable rate, making both options less than ideal. *Because of this uncertain financial landscape, wise investment strategies are more important now than ever.*

This unique situation requires fresh ideas and investment tools that haven't been relied on in the past. Investing the way your parents did will not pay off. The majority of investment ideas used by financial professionals in the 1990s aren't applicable to today's markets. That kind of investing will likely get you in trouble and compromise your retirement. Today, you need a better PLAN.

## HOW MUCH RISK ARE YOU EXPOSED TO?

Many investors don't know how much risk they are exposed to. It is helpful to organize your assets so you can have a clear understanding of how much of your money is at risk and how much is in safer holdings. This process starts with listing all your assets.

Let's take a look at the two kinds of money:

**Hope So Money** is, as the name indicates, money that you *hope* will be there when you need it. Hope So Money represents what you would like to get out of your investments. Examples of Hope So Money include:

- Stock market funds, including index funds
- Mutual funds
- Variable annuities
- Real estate investment trusts (REITs)

**Know So Money** is money that you know you can count on. It is safer money that isn't exposed to the level of volatility as the asset types noted above. You can more confidently count on having this money when you need it. Examples of Know So Money are:

- Government backed bonds
- Savings and checking accounts
- Fixed indexed annuities
- Certificates of deposit (CDs)
- Treasuries
- Money market accounts

> » *Roy had a modest brokerage account that he added to when he could. When he changed jobs a couple years ago, at age 58, Roy transferred his 401(k) assets into an IRA. Just a few years from retirement, he is now beginning to realize that nearly every dollar he has saved for retirement is subject to market risk.*
>
> *Intuitively, he knows that the time has come to shift some assets to an alternative that is safer, but how much is the right amount?*

## RULE OF 100

Determining the amount of risk that is right for you is dependent on a number of variables. You need to feel comfortable with where and how you are investing your money, and your financial professional is obligated to help you make decisions that put your money in places that fit your risk criteria.

Your retirement plan needs to first accommodate your day-to-day income needs. How much money do you need to maintain your lifestyle? When do you need it?

Managing your risk by having a balance of Hope So Money vs. Know So Money is a good start that will put you ahead of the curve. But how much Know So Money is enough to secure your income needs during retirement, and how much Hope So Money is enough to allow you to continue to benefit from an improving market?

In short, how do you begin to know how much risk you should be exposed to?

While there is no single approach to investment risk determination advice that is universally applicable to everyone, there are some helpful guidelines. One of the most useful is called *The Rule of 100.*

The average investor needs to accumulate assets to create a retirement plan that provides income during retirement and also allows for legacy planning. To accomplish this, they need to balance the amount of risk to which they are exposed. Risk is required because, while Know So Money is safer, more reliable and more dependable, it doesn't grow very fast, if at all. Today's historically low interest rates barely break even with current inflation. Hope So Money, while less dependable, has more potential for growth. Hope So Money can eventually become Know So Money once you move it to an investment with lower risk. Everyone's risk diversification will be different depending on their goals, age and their existing assets.

So how do you decide how much risk your assets should be exposed to? Where do you begin? Luckily, there's a guideline you can use to start making decisions about risk management. It's called the Rule of 100.

## THE RULE OF 100

The Rule of 100 is a general rule that helps shape asset diversification* for the average investor. The rule states that the number 100 minus an investor's age equals the amount of assets they should have exposed to risk.

> **The Rule of 100**: 100 - (your age) = the percentage of your assets that should be exposed to risk (Hope So Money)

For example, if you are a 30-year-old investor, the Rule of 100 would indicate that you should be focusing on investing primarily in the market and taking on a substantial amount of risk in your portfolio. The Rule of 100 suggests that 70 percent of your investments should be exposed to risk.

$$100 - (30 \text{ years of age}) = 70 \text{ percent}$$

Now, not every 30-year-old should have exactly 70 percent of their assets in mutual funds and stocks. The Rule of 100 is based on your chronological age, not your "financial age," which could vary based on your investment experience, your aversion or acceptance of risk and other factors. While this rule isn't an ironclad solution to anyone's finances, it's a pretty good place to start. Once you've taken the time to look at your assets with a professional to deter-

---

*Asset Diversification disclosure – Diversification and asset allocation does not assure or guarantee better performance and cannot eliminate the risk of investment loss. Before investing, you should carefully read the applicable volatility disclosure for each of the underlying funds, which can be found in the current prospectus.

mine your risk exposure, you can use the Rule of 100 to make changes that put you in a more stable investment position—one that reflects your comfort level.

Perhaps when you were age 30 and starting your career, like in the example above, it made sense to have 70 percent of your money in the market: you had time on your side. You had plenty of time to save more money, work more and recover from a downturn in the market. Retirement was ages away, and your earning power was increasing. And indeed, younger investors should take on more risk for exactly those reasons. The potential reward of long-term involvement in the market outweighs the risk of investing when you are young.

Risk tolerance generally reduces as you get older, however. If you are 40 years old and lose 30 percent of your portfolio in a market downturn this year, you have 20 or 30 years to recover it. If you are 68 years old, you have five to 10 years (or less) to make the same recovery. That new circumstance changes your whole retirement perspective. At age 68, it's likely that you simply aren't as interested in suffering through a tough stock market. There is less time to recover from downturns, and the stakes are higher. The money you have saved is money you will soon need to provide you with income, or is money that you already need to meet your income demands.

Much of the flexibility that comes with investing earlier in life is related to *compounding*. Compounded earnings can be incredibly powerful over time. The longer your money has time to compound, the greater your wealth will be. This is what most people talk about when they refer to putting their money to work. This is also why the Rule of 100 favors risk for the young. If you start investing when you are young, you can invest smaller amounts of money in a more aggressive fashion because you have the potential to make a profit in a rising market and you can harness the power of compounding earnings. When you are 40, 50 or 60 years old, that potential becomes less and less and you are forced to have more money at lower amounts of risk to realize the same returns. **It basically becomes more expensive to prudently invest the older you get.**

You risk not having a recovery period the older you get, so should have less of your assets at risk in volatile investments. You should shift with the Rule of 100 to protect your assets and ensure that they will provide you with the income you need in retirement. Let's look at another example that illustrates how the Rule of 100 becomes more critical as you age. An 80-year-old investor who is retired and is relying on retirement assets for income, for example, needs to depend on a solid amount of Know So Money. The Rule of 100 says an 80-year-old investor should have a maximum of 20 percent of his or her assets at risk. Depending on the investor's financial position, even less risk exposure may be required. You are the only person who can make this kind of determination, but the Rule of 100 can help. Everyone has their own level of comfort. Your Rule of 100 results will be based on your values and attitudes as well as your comfort with risk.

The Rule of 100 can apply to overarching financial management and to specific investment products that you own as well. Take the 401(k) for example. Many people have them, but not many people understand how their money is allocated within their 401(k). An employer may have someone who comes in once a year and explains the models and options that employees can choose from, but that's as much guidance as most 401(k) holders get. Many 401(k) options include target date funds that change their risk exposure over time, essentially following a form of the Rule of 100. Selecting one of these options can often be a good move for employees because they shift your risk as you age, securing more Know So Money when you need it.

A financial professional can look at your assets with you and discuss alternatives to optimize your balance between Know So and Hope So Money.

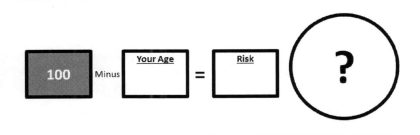

## CHAPTER 2 RECAP //

- Your retirement plan should be more nuanced than just a financial plan. A true retirement plan accounts for non-financial aspects, including your goals, fears, hopes, and specific desires. Ask yourself what you want to do during retirement, what you want that time to look like, and what you want it to feel like. How will you stay active, engaged, and healthy? What are some of your main goals and how will you achieve them?

- Some money you hope you'll have in the future. Some money you know you'll have in the future. Make sure you know how much you need to retire and when you will need it.

- Create a list to start organizing your assets. Identifying each asset can help you understand how it is balanced for risk and how you might want to adjust your portfolio to reflect you true tolerance for risk.

- You determine your own tolerance for risk, but there are some guidelines that can help you.

- The Rule of 100 can be a good starting point for understanding how much risk your portfolio is exposed to compared to how much is recommended for someone your age. You can use it as a starting point for determining your comfort with risk.

# 3

# THE COLORS OF YOUR MONEY

Going a step further, we can organize the types of investments and assets you have into a helpful visual schematic. Converting your portfolio of savings and investments in a lifetime stream of income, a legacy, and a successful retirement is an ambitious endeavor. Before the thought of it overwhelms you, it can be helpful to assign colors to your investments to keep them organized. Each color will represent the risk it is exposed to and will help you clarify the investment's purpose and potential. Viewing your assets in this light will give you an easy way to understand your portfolio and how it is working for you.

## THE COLOR OF MONEY
If you think of your retirement as a road trip, you can imagine how you would prepare for it. You need to pack the right things,

have accurate maps, reliable recommendations, and build in some time for fun and exploration. While you're on the road, you will encounter traffic, detours, and unexpected attractions. You'll also encounter traffic lights. Thinking of your investments and assets in terms of red, green, and yellow traffic signals is a good way to understand what they can mean for your retirement road trip.

**Green Money.** Green Money is your Know So Money. It is safer, more dependable, and easier to rely on. Assets in this category have built-in principal protection. This money will be there when you need it, and you can count on knowing that. Generally speaking, moving more of your assets into the Green Money category as you approach retirement can help protect your retirement income and the principal value of your investments. Green means go. These assets signal you can drive ahead with your plans knowing your principal is protected.

**Yellow Money.** Yellow Money is another type of safe Know So Money. These are liquid assets that you have access to whenever you need them. Having access to cash is an important consideration to take into account when crafting your retirement plan. Unplanned expenses like home improvements, car repairs, or family emergencies often require access to cash, and quickly. As a retiree, you may not have the option to work overtime to make some more cash, or pick up a shift somewhere to earn the money. Having access to liquid assets built in to your plan can help smooth the road during times when having access to cash is necessary. You don't want to take money from your income-generating assets, or other investments that are in the market or elsewhere. Besides the penalties you may incur, removing money from your active investments can diminish their potential for growth, which could affect your future plans, or put your future retirement income in jeopardy. Yellow Money doesn't earn big returns, but the flip side is that it is always available with no strings attached. This money is like a yellow traffic signal because you must proceed with caution:

if you allocate too much Yellow Money or use it unwisely, you run the risk of outliving your money.

**Red Money.** Red Money represents assets and investments that are exposed to risk. This is your Hope So Money because it doesn't come with a guarantee. It is exposed to market volatility and is vulnerable to economic changes. Like a red light at an intersection, you need to stop and consider how much money you can afford to expose to risk, how much growth potential your plan needs, and how red money assets affect your portfolio and your retirement plan as a whole. This money is affected by market upturns *and* downturns.

The colors of money are helpful ways to understand your investments, but they are not overall recommendations about what kind of investments are good or bad. There are no bad investments or assets: there are investments that help you achieve your goals, and ones that don't. The decisions you make about risk exposure can help you choose investments that match your goals. Working with a financial professional held to a fiduciary standard can help you make those decisions and position your money to fit your plan.

How much Green, Yellow, and Red Money do you need? That's up to you.

| Green Money | Red Money | Yellow Money |
|---|---|---|
| "Green Money" is safer. | "Red Money" is at risk. | "Yellow Money" represents liquid assets. |
| This is money that offers a minimum guarantee but it may pose risks other than market risk. | This is money that can go up or down in value. It may pose risk if it is not properly managed to serve a specific purpose in a comprehensive plan. | This safe, Know So Money is liquid and easily accessible. It gives you access to cash for emergencies. |

The fact of the matter is that a lot of people don't know their level of exposure to risk. Visually organizing your assets is an important and powerful way to get a clear picture of what kind of money you have, where it is and how you can best use it in the future. This process is as simple as listing your assets and assigning them a color based on their status as Know So or Hope So Money. Work with your financial professional to create a comprehensive inventory of your assets to understand what you are working with before making any decisions. This may be the first time you have ever sat down and sorted out all of your assets, allowing you to see how much money you have at risk in the market. Comparing the color of your investments will give you an idea of how near or far you are from adhering to the Rule of 100.

Over the course of your lifetime, it is likely that you have acquired a variety of assets. Assets can range from money that you have in a savings account or a 401(k), to a pension or an IRA. You have earned money and have made financial decisions based on the best information you had at the time. When viewed as a whole, however, you might not have an overall strategy for the management of your assets. As we have seen, it's more important than ever to know which of your assets are at risk. High market volatility and low treasury rates make for challenging financial topography. Navigating this financial landscape starts with planful asset management that takes into account your specific needs and options.

Even if you feel that you have plenty of money in your 401(k) or IRA, not knowing how much *risk* those investments are exposed to can cause you major financial suffering. Take the market crash of 2008 for example. In 2008, the average investor lost 30 percent of their 401(k). If more people had shifted their investments away from risk as they neared retirement age (i.e. the Rule of 100), they may have lost a lot less money going into retirement.

When using the Rule of 100 to calculate your level of risk, your financial age might be different than your chronological age, however. The way you organize your assets depends on your goals and your level of comfort with risk. Whatever you determine the appropriate amount of risk for you to be, you will need to organize your portfolio to reflect your goals. If you have more Red Money than Green Money, in particular, you will need to make decisions about how to move it. You can work with a financial professional to find appropriate Green Money options for your situation.

The next step is to know the right amount and ratio of Green and Red Money for you at your stage of retirement planning.

Investing heavily in Red Money and gambling all of your assets on the market is incredibly risky no matter where you fall within the Rule of 100. Money in the market can't be depended on to generate income, and a plan that leans too heavily on Red Money can easily fail, especially when investment decisions are influenced by emotional reactions to market downturns and recoveries. Not only is this an unwise plan, it can be incredibly stressful to an investor who is gambling everything on stocks and mutual funds.

But a plan that uses too much Green Money avoids all volatility and can also fail. Why? Investing all of your money in Certificates of Deposit (CDs), savings accounts, money markets and other low return accounts may provide interest and income, but that likely won't be enough to keep pace with inflation. If you focus exclusively on income from Green Money and avoid owning any stocks or mutual funds in your portfolio, you won't be able to leverage the potential for long-term growth your portfolio needs to stay healthy and productive. This is where the Rule of 100 can help you determine how much of your money should be invested in the market to anticipate your future needs.

Green Money becomes much more important as you age. While you want to reduce the amount of Red Money you have and to transition it to Green Money, you don't necessarily need all of it to generate income for you right away. Taking a closer look at Green Money, you will see there are actually different types.

## TYPES OF GREEN MONEY:
### *NEED NOW AND NEED LATER*

Money that you need to depend on for income is Green Money. Once you have filled the income gap at the beginning of your retirement, you may have money left over.

*There are two types of Green Money:* money used for income and money used for accumulation to meet your income needs in five, 10 or 20 years. Money needed for income is Need Now Money. It is money you need to meet your basic needs, to pay your bills, your mortgage if you have one and the costs associated with maintaining your lifestyle. Money used for accumulation is Need Later Money. It's money that you don't need now for income, but will need to rely on down the road. It's still Green Money because you will rely on it later for income and will need to count on it being there. Need Later Money represents income your assets will need to generate for future use. When planning your retirement, it is vital to decide how much of your assets to structure for income and how much to set aside to accumulate to create Need Later Money.

You must figure out if your income and accumulation needs are met. Your Need Now and Need Later Money are top priorities. Need Now Money, in particular, will dictate what your options for future needs are.

## OPTIMIZING RISK AND FINDING THE RIGHT BALANCE

Determining the amount of risk that is right for you depends on your specific situation. It starts by examining your particular financial position.

The Rule of 100 is a useful way to begin to deliberate the right amount of risk for you. But remember, it's just a baseline. Use it as a starting point for figuring out where your money should be. If you're a 50-year-old investor, the Rule of 100 suggests that you have 50 percent Green Money and 50 percent Red Money. Most 50-year-olds are more risk tolerant, however. There are many reasons why someone might be more risk tolerant, not the least of which is feeling young! Experienced investors, people who feel they need to gamble for a higher return, or people who have met their retirement income goals and are looking for additional ways to accumulate wealth are all candidates for investment strategies that incorporate higher levels of risk. In the end, it comes down to your personal tolerance for risk. How much are you willing to lose?

Consulting with a financial professional is often the wisest approach to calculating your risk level. A professional can help determine your risk tolerance by getting to know you, asking you a set of questions and even giving you a survey to determine your comfort level with different types of risk. Here's a typical scenario a financial professional might pose to you:

*"You have $100,000 saved that you would like to invest in the market. There is an investment product that could turn your $100,000 into $120,000. That same option, however, has the potential of losing you up to $30,000, leaving you with $70,000."*

Is that a scenario that you are willing to enter into? Or are you more comfortable with this one:

*"You could turn your $100,000 into $110,000, but have the potential of losing $15,000, leaving you with $85,000."*

Your answer to these and others types of questions will help a financial professional determine what level of risk is right for you. They can then offer you investment strategies and management plans that reflect your financial age.

## THE NUMBERS DON'T LIE

When the rubber meets the road, the numbers dictate your options. Your risk tolerance is an important indicator of what kinds of investments you should consider, but if the returns from those investments don't meet your retirement goals, your income needs will likely not be met. For example, if the level of risk you are comfortable with manages your investments at a 4 percent return and you need to realize an 8 percent return, your income needs aren't going to be met when you need to rely on your investments for retirement income. A professional may encourage you to be more aggressive with your investment strategy by taking on more risk in order to give you the potential of earning a greater return.

Many investors who are used to exposing their assets to risk may focus more on the potential for gain and the rate of return instead of the security of their dependable income. They may allocate more of their portfolio in Red Money investments, betting on a market upswing and big profits, when a Green Money investment might be more suitable by generating income from a steady, dependable investment with a more predictable rate of return.

Again, a financial professional can help you design and enact a plan that meets your long-term needs. They can show you where exposure to risk is unnecessary for some goals, and advisable for others.

How are you going to structure your income flow during retirement? The answer to this question dictates how you determine your risk tolerance. You might be surprised by how little risk you have to take on to achieve your goals. Look at the numbers to see what kind of risk allocation you really need to get the retirement you want.

## HOW TO INTERVIEW A FINANCIAL PROFESSIONAL

You won't have trouble finding a financial professional. There are plenty of people eager to work with investors and people planning for retirement. The problem isn't finding someone—the problem is finding the *right* someone. It's important to know that the person you are working with is making decisions based on your best interests, isn't simply trying to sell you products, and isn't working with you just for the money. These questions can help you sort out who wants to work with you and who doesn't.

**How do you earn your paycheck?** This may seem like an unnecessarily personal question, but it gets to the heart of a very important matter. Commission-based professionals get paid for what they sell. They are motivated to sell financial products to earn more money. Fee-based professionals, like Registered Investment Advisors (RIAs) earn fees for their services based on a flat percentage of the managed asset. The difference may seem small at first, but it is an important distinction.

**What experience do you have?** This can be revealed through a conversation, a resume, or both. It is important to know where your financial professional is coming from, what background they have, and how it has shaped the way they view investing and retirement planning.

**What can you offer me / how can you help me?** You aren't just looking for someone to shuffle papers for you and make phone calls. You need a professional who acts in your best interest, shows you your options, and empowers you to achieve your goals. You need a strategist and someone you can trust. If they can only offer you transactional services, they may not be the best choice for you and the ambitious planning process that lies ahead of you.

## MORE ON PAYMENT

It is helpful to understand what motivates the person you choose to work with. Understanding the differences between commission-based payment and fee-based payment can help reveal these motivations. The choices a financial professional makes and the things they recommend can be strongly influenced by the way they are paid.

**Commissions.** Brokers, registered representatives, and other types of financial professionals are paid on commission. When they sell a product their company offers, they get paid for it. The products they sell aren't inherently bad or good. They are financial products, and not plans, however. The distinction is important. These professionals are held to suitability standards of liability, which means the products they recommend must be considered suitable for an investor. This can be broadly interpreted, and is not a reliable way to build a retirement plan. Additionally, a product that made sense for you in your 40s might not make sense for you in your late 50s, after a large market correction, or after you have a grandchild. There is little to no incentive for commission-based professionals to update your plan or adjust it to benefit you. They are motivated by selling individual products to earn money.

**Fees.** RIAs are paid by fees for services. They earn a flat percentage of the assets they manage, tying their success to yours. Additionally, RIAs are independent professionals who are not limited to financial products sold by one company. They operate under fiduciary standards of liability, meaning their recommendations must not only suitable for a particular investor, but must be made in their best interest. They also look out for your heirs' best interest. They cannot make recommendations that prioritize their potential for profit over your potential for successful planning and investing. This model incentivizes them to stay in touch with, update your plan and your portfolio throughout your life, and to truly understand your goals for investing and for retirement.

Planning a retirement requires careful consideration. A quality financial planner creates a fully functioning plan for you that is larger than the sum of its parts. Instead of a set of individual financial products and investments, a planner will help you create a *plan* that helps all aspects of your portfolio work together to achieve your goals.

You might have two million dollars stored away in a savings account, but your neighbor, who has $300,000 in a diverse investment portfolio that is tailored to their needs, may end up enjoying a better retirement lifestyle. Why? They had more than a good work ethic and a penchant for saving. They had a planful approach to retirement asset allocation.

## CHAPTER 3 RECAP //

- Organizing your investments by color can help you understand how much risk they are exposed to and how they can work to help you achieve your planning goals. Think of your assets in terms of Green, Yellow, and Red Money. Green Money represents assets that are "safer" and more reliable. Red Money represents assets that are exposed to risk. Yellow Money represents liquid assets you have direct access to that is available for emergencies and unexpected expenses.

- There are two types of Green Money: *Need Now and Need Later*. It is important to structure your investments to provide you with income now and later.

- Working with a Registered Investment Advisor will help you compose a clear and concise inventory of your assets, and learn how much they are worth, what rules apply to them, and how they are structured for risk.

- The way a financial professional is paid can shed light on their motivations. RIAs held to fiduciary standards of liability are required to make recommendations in your best interest. Because they are compensated through a fee-based model, their success is tied to your success.

# 4

# CREATING A LIFETIME OF INCOME

*How much money do you need to retire?*

An important aspect of your financial plan is the evaluation of your income needs. Finding the most efficient and beneficial way to address them will have impacts on your lifestyle, your asset accumulation and your legacy planning after you retire. When you have identified your income need, you will know how much to structure for income and how much to be set aside for accumulation.

***Every financial strategy for retirement needs first to accommodate the day-to-day need for income.*** The moment your working income ceases and you start living off the money you've set aside for retirement is referred to as the **retirement cliff**. When you begin drawing income from your retirement assets, you have entered the distribution phase of your financial plan. ***The distribution phase of your retirement plan*** is when you reach the point of relying on your assets for income. This is where your Green Money comes into play: the safer, more reliable assets that you have accumulated that are designed to provide you with a steady income. On day one of your retirement, you will need a steady and reliable supply of income from your Green Money.

Satisfying that need for daily income entails first knowing ***how much you need*** and ***when you will need it.***

**How Much Money Do You Need?** The amount of money you need isn't a number we can pull out of the air. We need accurate information based on consistent data. The best way to achieve that input is by creating an accurate budget. It's never something that sounds fun, but it's a crucial step in figuring out how to create a plan to truly meet your needs. A budget doesn't mean you have to restrict yourself during retirement. It is a window into your spending life that will help you structure an income that gives you what you need to maintain or improve your lifestyle in retirement.

While this amount will be different for everyone, the general rule of thumb is that a retiree will require 70 to 80 percent of their pre-retirement income to maintain their lifestyle. This isn't always the case, however. Many people anticipate spending needs that meet or exceed their previous budget. This increase can be reflected in more travel, large expenses you've been waiting for until retirement, and more involvement with hobbies or community activities. When you arrive at a number that reflects your needs, you can start doing the work of adjusting your portfolio and creating a plan that helps you generate the income you need.

**When Do You Need Your Money?** If you need income to last 10 years, use a tool that creates just that. If you need a lifetime of income, seek a tool that will do that and won't run out.

So how do you figure out how much you need and when you need it? When you take health care costs, potential emergencies, plans for moving or traveling, and other retirement expenses into account, you can really give your calculator a workout. You want to maximize retirement benefits to meet your lifetime income needs. An Investment Advisor can help you answer those questions by working with you to customize an income plan.

## PLANNING FOR SPOUSAL CONTINUATION

Retirement income planning for married couples needs to take the possibility of the loss of a spouse into consideration. No one wants to talk about it, but it is an important reality that you should plan for. No one can prevent the death of a spouse, but you can create a plan that helps secure sufficient income for the survivor. The fact of the matter is that even with one less person in the household, expenses rarely go down. The death of a spouse can reduce your income, but not the expense of your lifestyle. You still have the house payment, the heating bill, taxes, and other expenses related to family and travel.

One of the building blocks of your retirement income is your Social Security benefit. The spousal benefit option allows the surviving spouse to choose the larger of the two benefit checks after their husband or wife passes away. This allows you to maximize your income from Social Security and can improve your chances of maintaining sufficient income to support your lifestyle. Before you get there, however, it's important to create a maximization strategy that will take the fullest advantage of your Social Security filing options to pay you the highest lifetime amount. You may not know about filing strategies, or you may have a general idea about when it is "smart" to file. Until you sit down with a professional planner and determine your specific circumstances with a maximization report, you don't really know.

Other investment tools are specifically designed for spousal continuation. You may want to consider them as you make your retirement plan. Investment options like life insurance policies, and hybrid annuities with income and death benefit riders can help protect you or your spouse from a loss of income should one of you pass away. We'll get more in depth about these options in the chapters to ahead.

One of the biggest takeaways regarding spousal continuation and building it into your plan is that both spouses need to be informed and involved in the retirement planning process. If one person is solely in charge of the paperwork and decision-making, it can set you up for confusion, frustration, and grief when the other spouse needs to figure everything out from square one. Make sure you both understand your plan, your spousal continuation plan, and where the money is coming from.

As we determined in earlier chapters, the most important thing you need to do as you create an income plan is to take care to avoid too much exposure to risk. You can start by meeting with an Investment Advisor to organize your assets. Get your Green Money and Red Money in order and balanced to meet your needs. If the market goes down 18 percent this afternoon, you don't want that to come out of what you're relying on for next year's income. Hot on the heels of securing your Green Money, it's time to structure those Green Money assets so they can generate income for you. Ultimately, you have to take care of your monthly income needs to pay the bills.

The Big Kahuna of Green Money is your Social Security benefit.

## CHAPTER 4 RECAP //

- You need to know how much money you need for a successful retirement, and when you need it. This is the foundation of your retirement income strategy.
- Spousal continuation should be built in to your retirement plan. When one of you passes away, the surviving spouse could face the potential loss of income. It is hard enough to lose a loved one. Proper planning can protect you from losing income and stability, as well. Make sure you both understand your finances and your retirement plan so you are prepared for the future.
- Filing for Social Security benefits can have a huge impact on your income plan. Be aware that maximizing your Social Security benefit can be done with the help of a financial professional and it can save you thousands of dollars over the course of your retirement.

# 5
# WOMEN IN RETIREMENT

Planning for retirement today is a difficult task for anyone. Women have a particularly unique set of challenges ahead of them, however. Creating a durable, lasting retirement plan that takes these challenges into account is essential for any woman entering retirement. Women are often faced with having to make financial decisions due to the death of a spouse, a divorce, or because they choose to focus on their career. Many women lack confidence while making these decisions, however. Coupled with being more risk-averse and earning less (on average) than men, many women will face an income loss that will need to be addressed in their retirement plan.

According to the Women's Institute for Financial Education (WIFE), 50 percent of marriages end in divorce and 35 percent end in widowhood. On average, women spend a third of their adult life on their own, financially. Unfortunately, we don't learn the ins and outs of personal finance in grammar school, high school or even at the collegiate level. Most people learn about finances by watching how it is handled in their family (i.e., how their father handled the money). Today, women are making financial decisions even though they were never properly taught about how to handle their finances. This lack of education and confidence leaves many women struggling to replace the income gap when there is a loss of income.

If you are a woman preparing to retire, ask yourself the following questions:

- Where have I been getting retirement advice? Why? Your spouse, your friends, and your plumber can all have opinions about how you should invest your money or organize your finances. Consider speaking with a registered investment advisor who is legally obligated to protect your best interests in financial matters.
- Is my legacy secure? Do I have a solid plan for my legacy to pass to my children or other beneficiaries?
- What assets do I own, and why? In order to create a useful plan, you need to know what you have to work with, and how it can work for you. When you have a clear understanding of what makes up your portfolio, you can make informed decisions about your financial future.
- Do I have enough income to last my lifetime?
- What is my net worth? Your net worth is a starting point for knowing what your options are. You can determine your net worth by subtracting your liabilities from your assets.
- Can I retire free of debt? This may sound like a difficult task, but retiring without debt can help you minimize your liabilities and strengthen your overall financial position. In the event you need long-term care or face some

other unexpected financial burden, being free of debt can put you in a position to have more options, and give you peace of mind.

Understanding your finances and your financial goals is the first step toward providing yourself with income and stability during retirement. Answering these questions will put you ahead of the game and put you on track to make decisions that will set you up for success.

## THE CHALLENGES WOMEN FACE IN RETIREMENT

Retirement has different realities in store for women and men. Women should be prepared to find solutions that fit their needs. Life expectancies, pension considerations, and health care needs, along with many other factors, often vary between men and women. All of these things affect how you should make decisions regarding your retirement. Consider the following factors:

- **Life expectancy**. Wives typically outlive their husbands by six years.* This often means women are left to live with the financial decisions their husbands have made. By being involved in your finances throughout your life, you can prevent surprises or unpleasant financial realities in the future. It is also important to work with a financial professional you trust who is obligated to make decisions and recommendations in your best interest. Among the challenges a surviving spouse can face are reduced Social Security benefits, reduced or eliminated pension payments, and taxable events.
- **Healthcare**. It is impossible to know exactly how much you will need to spend on health care during retirement. Long-term care is an increasing reality for many women

---

* *http://www.scientificamerican.com/article.cfm?id=why-women-live-longer*

due to their longer life expectancies. Your retirement plan should address this reality. It is important to protect your retirement income from these potential costs. Many women have not included this step in their retirement plans, however. Additionally, long-term care needs for your spouse can also pose a serious threat to your retirement income. Protect your savings and the stability of your retirement with a plan to pay health care costs.

- **Pensions**. Pensions are not as common as they once were, and not everyone can rely on one for income during retirement. If you or your spouse have or will have income from a pension, it is important to understand them terms of the pension. Married women often experience the loss of pension income when their spouse passes away. Without adequate survivorship options in place, all or most of the pension income can disappear. By understanding your pension income and your survivorship options, you can prevent this from happening. Taking the right steps for your situation begins with educating yourself about the pensions you have in your life.

- **Destination**. What do you want your retirement to look and feel like? What do you want to do, and how do you want to spend your time? Taking the time to visualize your retired life can help you make decisions that help you achieve those goals. If you don't know where you are going, it will be difficult to get there. When you know what you want, you can begin selecting the financial tools to help you build your retirement reality.

## FINANCIAL PLANNING FOR WOMEN

Good financial planning can help women overcome the unique challenges they face in retirement. To create a useful plan, women should address the variables that affect their financial realities. The following steps can help you address the potential pitfalls that lie ahead before you encounter them.

## Step 1
### Determine the level of financial risk you are comfortable with.

Everyone has a different tolerance for risk. Age, net worth, income, and familiarity with investing all affect how comfortable someone is with risk. The Rule of 100 can help you find your baseline risk level, and from there you can determine what level you feel best at. This information is important because it helps you make decisions about your financial plan. Most importantly, you can begin allocating the assets in your portfolio to reflect the level of risk you are comfortable with. Organizing your financial life in this manner will give you peace of mind and provide a cornerstone for your retirement.

### Consider the following types of assets as you determine what is right for you:

- Property assets. Owning property requires maintenance, taxes, insurance payments, and occupancy management (with rental properties). The sale of property can trigger significant taxable events, as well. Real estate is often considered a Red Money asset for these reasons.
- Equity assets. These investments include stocks, and they require careful monitoring. Are you qualified and willing to spend the time and energy necessary to manage equity assets while you are enjoying retirement?
- Fixed Assets. Have you met your income needs with reliable assets? If most of your money is in the bank, it may not even be keeping up with inflation. You can work with a financial professional to find safe and insured invest-

ment options that can generate lasting and dependable monthly income.

## Step 2
### Find an advisor you can trust.

Your retirement plan is one of the most important things in your life. It affects your future and the future of your loved ones. It is important to find a financial professional you can trust and who is obligated to make recommendations in your best interest. This decision isn't about whether or not you like someone, but whether or not you can trust them. There are many types of financial professionals that claim to be comprehensive retirement planners, but not everyone is required to give you advice that is in your best interest.

Unlike brokers and insurance-only agents, only Registered Investment Advisors are held to a fiduciary standard. Instead of being paid commissions for transactions and sales of financial products, RIAs are typically compensated by a fee based on the amount of assets they manage for you. You can protect yourself by taking the time to find an RIA you trust and connect with. Make sure to ask all of the questions you have, and make sure you feel comfortable with the person you meet with before deciding to trust them with your retirement.

## Step 3
### Secure your income.

The difference between the amount of money you can depend on for income each month and the amount you need to maintain your lifestyle and meet your expenses is called the income gap. When you need more than you have, you are dealing with a gap, and something needs to fill it, or something needs to make it smaller.

Unfortunately, many married women become impoverished when their husbands die.* The reason is a sudden loss of dependable income, usually from Social Security benefits and pensions. Women stand to lose the most income in the event of a spouse passing. It is true that a widow can select to receive her husband's Social Security benefit amount if it was higher than her own, but she may still be living with a net income reduced by 40 to 80 percent.

You can protect yourself and your income by building guaranteed income-generating assets into your retirement plan. One type of asset that can provide you with guaranteed income is an annuity. There are more annuity options today than ever, and you can use them to create a kind of "personalized pension" that will pay you an income while protecting the value of your asset at the same time.

## Step 4
### Consider Stretch IRA options.
Stretch IRA options can help you do just what the name implies: stretch the value of your or your spouse's IRA. In 1986, Congress passed the Tax Reform Act, allowing multi-generational distributions for IRA assets. A Stretch IRA can extend distributions throughout yours, your children's and your grandchildren's lifetimes.

## Step 5
### Prepare your legacy and plan for the passage of your estate.
You can have control over your legacy by making comprehensive plans. The more you prepare, the more efficient the process will be, ensuring your wishes are carried out with accuracy.

---

* *https://www.ssa.gov/policy/docs/ssb/v65n3/v65n3p31.html*

The following questions can help you begin the process:
- Are your beneficiary forms up to date? The beneficiary form takes precedence over last will and testaments, trusts and divorce decrees.
- Have you initiated important legacy planning documents?
- Does it allow the multi-generational payout?
- Do you have a will?
- Have you set up a power of attorney?
- Have you provided a trust and guardianship for minor children?
- Have you selected an estate administrator?
- Do you know where your important documents are located?
- Do you have primary and contingent beneficiaries?
- Do you know what benefits are available to you from the social security administration?

## Step 6
**Get a second opinion.**
You don't always strike oil the first place you drill. Seeking a second (or third) opinion from someone who has experience and expertise working with women can help you find the professional who is right for you.

These guidelines can help you feel confident about your retirement, and can make a huge difference in your financial future. The most important element is being informed about your finances and the consequences that could lie ahead. Your retirement is an ongoing process, and an experience you should enjoy. Take care of your finances, and your finances will take care of you.

## CHAPTER 5 RECAP //

- Women have a unique set of considerations and challenges to deal with when preparing for retirement.
- Take the time to educate yourself about the potential consequences and realities that lie ahead in your financial future.
- Seek advice from a professional you can trust who will make recommendations based on your best interest.

# 6
# CREATING A SOCIAL SECURITY MAXIMIZATION REPORT

*When is the right time to file for benefits?*

One kind of Green Money that most Americans rely on for income when they retire is Social Security. If you're like most Americans, Social Security is or will be an important part of your retirement income and one that you should know how to properly manage. As a first step in creating your income plan, a financial professional will take a look at your Social Security benefit options. The keystone of your strategy is the Social Security Maximization Report. Your financial professional will have access to proprietary software that makes the complex calculations of filing time, life expectancy, and other factors, showing you how to get the most from your benefit. The options and filing strategies available to you, especially if you're married, can save you thousands of dollars over your retirement. Your report will clearly list all of your filing options and the dollar advantage of each one so you can easily see and understand each one. Your Social Security benefit is a critical part of your retirement income. It is an important source of reliable Green Money, and you need to take the time to seek the detailed guidance a personalized report can give you.

> » Patricia had worked full-time nearly her entire adult life and was looking forward to enjoying retirement with her husband, kids and grandkids. When she turned 62, she decided to take advantage of her Social Security benefits as soon as they became available.
>
> A couple of years later, she was organizing some of the paperwork in her home office. She came across an old Social Security statement, and remembered the feeling of filing and beginning a new phase in her life.
>
> However, as she looked over the statement, she realized in retrospect that she might have been better off waiting to file for benefits. She had saved enough to wait for benefits, and if she had, her monthly benefit could have been quite a bit more.
>
> When she was in the process of retiring, there were so many other decisions to make. It seemed very straightforward to file right away. She made a note to call the Social Security Administration to see if it was possible to change her monthly benefit to the larger amount.

Here are some facts that illustrate how Americans currently use Social Security:

- Nearly 90 percent of Americans age 65 and older receive Social Security benefits.*
- Social Security provides about 34 percent of the income of the elderly.*
- Claiming Social Security benefits at the wrong time can reduce your monthly benefit by up to 65 percent.**
- In 2013, more than a third of workers claimed Social Security benefits as soon they became eligible.***
- In 2016, the average monthly Social Security benefit was $1,341. *The maximum benefit for 2016 was $2,639. The $1,298 monthly benefit reduction between the average and the maximum is applied for life.*****

There are many aspects of Social Security that are well known and others that aren't. When it comes time for you to cash in on your Social Security benefit, you will have many options and choices. Social Security is a massive government program that manages retirement benefits for millions of people. Experts spend their entire careers understanding and analyzing it. Luckily, you don't have to understand all of the intricacies of Social Security to maximize its advantages. You simply need to know the best way to manage your Social Security benefit. You need to know exactly what to do to get the most from your Social Security benefit and when to do it. Taking the time to create a roadmap for your Social Security strategy will help ensure that you are able to exact your maximum benefit and efficiently coordinate it with the rest of your retirement plan.

---

* *https://www.ssa.gov/news/press/factsheets/basicfact-alt.pdf*
** *https://www.ssa.gov/planners/retire/retirechart.html*
*** *Trends in Social Security Claiming, Alicia H Munnell and Anqi Chen, Center for Retirement Research, May 2015. http://crr.bc.edu/wp-content/uploads/2015/05/ IB_15-8.pdf*
**** *https://www.ssa.gov/news/press/factsheets/colafacts2016.html*

There are many aspects of Social Security that you have no control over. You don't control how much you put into it, and you don't control what it's invested in or how the government manages it. However, you do control when and how you file for benefits. The real question about Social Security that you need to answer is, "When should I start taking Social Security?" While this is the all-important question, there are a couple of key pieces of information you need to track down first.

Before we get into a few calculations and strategies that can make all the difference, let's start by covering the basic information about Social Security which should give you an idea of where you stand. Just as the foundation of a house creates the stable platform for the rest of the framework to rest upon, your Social Security benefit is an important part of your overall retirement plan. The purpose of the information that follows is not to give an exhaustive explanation of how Social Security works, but to give you some tools and questions to start understanding how Social Security affects your retirement and how you can prepare for it.

Let's start with eligibility.

**Eligibility.** Understanding how and when you are eligible for Social Security benefits will help clarify what to expect when the time comes to claim them.

To receive retirement benefits from Social Security, you must earn eligibility. In almost all cases, Americans born after 1929 must earn 40 quarters of credit to be eligible to draw their Social Security retirement benefit. In 2016, a Social Security credit represents $1,260 earned in a calendar quarter. The number changes as it is indexed each year, but not drastically. In 2015, a credit represented $1,220. Four quarters of credit is the maximum number that can be earned each year. In 2016, an American would have had to earn at least $5,040 to accumulate four credits. In order to qualify for retirement benefits, you must have earned a minimum number of credits. Although 40 is the minimum number of credits required to begin drawing benefits, it is important to know that once you claim your Social Security benefit, you are essentially locked into that base benefit amount forever. Additionally, if you are at least 62 years old, have been married for at least 12 months, and your spouse is currently collecting his or her own retirement benefit, then you can choose to receive Spousal Benefits based on your spouse's work record.

**Primary Insurance Amount.** Your primary insurance amount (PIA) is the dollar amount your monthly benefit will be when you reach your full retirement age (FRA). In other words, your PIA represents 100 percent of the monthly benefit to which you are entitled. If you opt to take benefits before your FRA, your monthly benefit will be less than your PIA. If you opt to delay taking benefits past your FRA, however, your monthly benefit will be more than your PIA. For example, if you filed at age 62, your monthly benefit would be 75 percent of your PIA. But if you waited to file until you were 70 years old and your FRA was age 66, your benefit would be 132 percent of your PIA. When it comes to filing for Social Security, timing is everything. You can think of your Social Security benefit as a ripening fruit—the goal is to pick the fruit when you can get the most out of it. If you file for benefits too early, you will be locked into receiving a monthly benefit amount less than the full amount to which you are entitled—you will essentially be picking an unripe fruit. On the other hand, the longer you wait to file the more your monthly benefit will increase, but every month you wait is one less check you'll get from the government—you don't want to wait too long and let the fruit become overripe.

**Full Retirement Age.** Your FRA is an important figure for anyone who is planning to rely on Social Security benefits in their retirement. Depending on when you were born, there is a specific age at which you will attain FRA. Your FRA is dictated by your year of birth and is the age at which you can begin receiving your

PIA. Your FRA is important because it is half of the equation used to calculate your Social Security benefit. The other half of the equation is based on when you start taking benefits.

When Social Security was initially set up, the FRA was age 65, and it still is for people born before 1938. But as time has passed, the age for receiving full retirement benefits has increased. If you were born between 1938 and 1960, your full retirement age is somewhere on a sliding scale between 65 and 67. Anyone born in 1960 or later will now have to wait until age 67 for full benefits. Increasing the FRA has helped the government reduce the cost of the Social Security program, which paid out almost $918 billion to beneficiaries in 2016!*

While you can begin collecting retirement benefits as early as age 62, the amount you receive as a monthly benefit will be less than it would be if you wait until you reach or surpass your FRA. It is important to note that if you file for your Social Security benefit before your FRA, *the reduction to your monthly benefit will remain in place for the rest of your life.* You can also delay receiving benefits up to age 70, in which case your benefits will be higher than your PIA for the rest of your life.

- At FRA, 100 percent of PIA is available as a monthly benefit.
- At age 62, your Social Security retirement benefits are available. For each month you take benefits prior to your FRA, however, the monthly amount of your benefit is reduced. *This reduction stays in place for the rest of your life.*
- At age 70, your monthly benefit reaches its maximum. After you turn age 70, your monthly benefit will no longer increase.

---

* *https://www.ssa.gov/news/press/factsheets/basicfact-alt.pdf*

| Year of Birth | Full Retirement Age |
|---|---|
| 1943-1954 | 66 |
| 1955 | 66 and 2 months |
| 1956 | 66 and 4 months |
| 1957 | 66 and 6 months |
| 1958 | 66 and 8 months |
| 1959 | 66 and 10 months |
| 1960 or later | age 67* |

## ROLLING UP YOUR SOCIAL SECURITY

Your Social Security income "rolls up" the longer you wait to claim it. Your monthly benefit will continue to increase until you turn 70 years old. Even though Social Security is the foundation of most people's retirement, many Americans feel that they don't have control over how or when they receive their benefits. The truth is that every dollar you increase your Social Security income by means less money you will have to spend from your nest egg to meet your retirement income needs, but many retirees do not take advantage of this fact. For many people, creating their Social Security strategy is the most important decision they can make to positively impact their retirement. ***The difference between the best and worst Social Security decision can be tens of thousands of dollars over a lifetime of benefits.***

**Deciding NOW or LATER:** Following the above logic, it makes sense to wait as long as you can to begin receiving your Social Security benefit. However, the answer isn't always that simple. Not everyone has the option of waiting. Many people need to rely on Social Security on day one of their retirement. Some might need the income. Others might be in poor health and don't feel they will live long enough to make waiting until their FRA worth-

---

* *http://www.ssa.gov/OACT/progdata/nra.html*

while for themselves or their families. It is also possible, however, that the majority of folks taking an early benefit at age 62 are simply under-informed about Social Security. Perhaps they make this major decision based on rumors and emotion.

**File Immediately if You:**
- Find your job is unbearable.
- Are willing to sacrifice retirement income.
- Are not healthy and need a reliable source of income.
- Are not concerned about increasing your survivor or dependent benefits.

**Consider Delaying Your Benefit if You:**
- Want to maximize your retirement income.
- Want to increase retirement benefits for your spouse.
- Are still working and like it.
- Are healthy and willing / able to wait to file.

So if you decide to wait, how long should you wait? Lots of people can put it off for a few years, but not everyone can wait until they are 70 years old. Your individual circumstances may be able to help you determine when you should begin taking Social Security. If you do the math, you will quickly see that between ages 62 and 70, there are 96 months in which you can file for your Social Security benefit. If you take into account those 96 months and the 96 months your spouse could also file for Social Security, and the number of different strategies for structuring your benefit, you can easily end up with more than 20,000 different scenarios. It's safe to say this isn't the kind of math that most people can easily handle. Each month would result in a different benefit amount. The longer you wait, the higher your monthly benefit amount becomes. Each month you wait, however, is one less month that you receive a Social Security check.

*The goal is to get the most out of your benefit.* That may not always mean waiting until you can get the largest monthly payment. Taking the bigger picture into account, you want to find out how to get the most money out of Social Security over the number of years that you draw from it. Don't underestimate the power of optimizing your benefit: the difference between the BEST and WORST Social Security election can easily be worth thousands of dollars in lifetime benefits. *The difference can be very substantial!*

If you know that every month you wait, your Social Security benefit goes up a little bit, and you also know that every month you wait, you receive one less benefit check, how do you determine where the sweet spot is that maximizes your benefits over your lifetime? Financial professionals have access to software that will calculate the best year and month for you to file for benefits based on your default life expectancy. You can further customize that information by estimating your life expectancy based on your health, habits and family history. If you can then create an income plan (we'll get into this later in the chapter) that helps you wait until the target date for you to file for Social Security, you can optimize your retirement income strategy to get the most out of your Social Security benefit. How can you calculate your life expectancy? Well, you don't know exactly how long you'll live, but you have a better idea than the government does. They rely on averages to make their calculations. *You have much more personal information about your health, lifestyle and family history than they do.* You can use that knowledge to game the system and beat all the other people who are making uninformed decisions by filing early for Social Security.

While you can and should educate yourself about how Social Security works, the reality is you don't need to know a lot of general information about Social Security in order to make choices about your retirement. What you do need to know is exactly

***what to do to maximize your benefit.*** Because knowing what you need to do has huge impacts on your retirement! For most Americans, Social Security is the foundation of income planning for retirement. Social Security benefits represent about 39 percent of the income of the elderly.* For many people, it can represent the largest portion of their retirement income. Not treating your Social Security benefit as an asset and investment tool can lead to sub-optimization of your largest source of retirement income.

Let's take a look at an example that shows the impact of working with a financial professional to optimize Social Security benefits:

> *» Preston and Shelly Valson are a typical American couple who have worked their whole lives and saved when they could. Preston is 60 years old, and Shelly is 56 years old. They sat down with a financial professional who logged onto the Social Security website to look up their PIAs. Preston's PIA is $1,900 and Shelly's is $900.*
>
> *If the Valsons cash in at age 62 and begin taking retirement benefits from Social Security, they will receive an estimated $568,600 in lifetime benefits. That may seem like a lot, but if you divide that amount over 20 years, it averages out to around $28,400 per year. The Valsons are accustomed to a more significant annual income than that. To make up the difference, they will have to rely on alternative retirement income options. They will basically have to depend on a bigger nest egg to provide them with the income they need.*
>
> *If they wait until their FRA, they will increase their lifetime benefits to an estimated $609,000. This option allows them to achieve their Primary Insurance Amount, which will provide them a $34,200 annual income.*

---

* *http://www.socialsecurity.gov/pressoffice/basicfact.htm*

> *After learning the Valsons' needs and using software to calculate the most optimal time to begin drawing benefits, the Valsons' financial professional determined that the best option for them drastically increases their potential lifetime benefits to $649,000!*
>
> *By using strategies that their financial professional recommended, they increased their potential lifetime benefits by as much as **$80,000**. There's no telling how much you could miss out on from your Social Security if you don't take time to create a strategy that calculates your maximum benefit. For the Valsons, the value of maximizing their benefits was the difference between night and day. While this may seem like a special case, it isn't uncommon to find benefit increases of this magnitude. You'll never know unless you take a look at your own options.*

Despite the importance of knowing when and how to take your Social Security benefit, many of today's retirees and pre-retirees may know little about the mechanics of Social Security and how they can maximize their benefit.

So, to whom should you turn for advice when making this complex decision? Before you pick up the phone and call Uncle Sam, you should know that Social Security Administration representatives are actually prohibited from giving you election advice! Plus, Social Security Administration representatives in general are trained to focus on monthly benefit amounts, not the lifetime income for a family.

## MAXIMIZING YOUR LIFETIME BENEFIT

As discussed in Chapter 2, calculating how to maximize **lifetime benefits** is more important than waiting until age 70 for your maximum **monthly benefit amount.** It's about getting the most income during your lifetime. Professional benefit maximization software can target the year and month that it is most beneficial for you to file based on your life expectancy.

The three most common ages that people associate with retirement benefits are 62 (Earliest Eligible Age), 66 (Full Retirement Age), and 70 (age at which monthly maximum benefit is reached). In almost all circumstances, however, none of those three most common ages will give you the maximum lifetime benefit.

Remember, every month you wait to file, the amount of your benefit check goes up, but you also get one less check. You don't know how exactly how long you're going to live, but you have a better idea of your life expectancy than the actuaries at the Social Security Administration who can only work with averages. They can't make calculations based on your specific situation. A professional can run the numbers for you and get the target date that maximizes your potential lifetime benefits. You can't get this information from the Social Security Administration, but you *can* get it from a financial professional.

**Types of Social Security Benefits:**
- *Retired Worker Benefit.* This is the benefit with which most people are familiar. The Retired Worker Benefit is what most people are talking about when they refer to Social Security. It is your benefit based on your earnings and the amount that you have paid into the system over the span of your career.
- *Spousal Benefit.* This is available to the spouse of someone who is eligible for Retired Worker Benefits.
- Survivorship Benefit. When one spouse passes away, the survivor is able to receive the larger of the two benefit amounts.
- *Restricted Application.* A higher-earning spouse may be able to start collecting a spousal benefit on the lower-earning spouse's benefit while allowing his or her benefit

to continue to grow. Due to the Bipartisan Budget Act of 2015, this option is only available to individuals who turned age 62 on or before January 1, 2016.

In November of 2015, the Bipartisan Budget Act of 2015 was passed, which will have a dramatic impact on the way many Americans plan for Social Security. As the largest change to Social Security since 2000, the Bipartisan Budget Act of 2015 eliminated an estimated $9.5 billion* of benefits to retirees and may limit some of the flexibility you previously had to structure your benefits.

In 2000, Congress passed the Senior Citizens Freedom to Work Act. The bill allowed retirees to suspend receiving benefits so they wouldn't be subject to additional taxation if they chose to return to work after they filed for Social Security. However, by doing so, the bill also unintentionally created several loopholes in claiming strategies: most notably, the Restricted Application for spousal benefits and "file and suspend" filing strategy. For most Americans, the Bipartisan Budget Act of 2015 closed these loopholes by eliminating "file and suspend" and the Restricted Application.

The new rules mandate that:

- If a primary worker is not currently receiving benefits, then their dependents (child, spouse) can no longer collect benefits based on the primary worker's earning record.
- If you file for benefits, then you are filing for *all* benefits to which you are entitled—not just the benefit type you choose.

---

* *http://www.nasdaq.com/article/congress-planning-to-close-social-security-loopholes-cm536252*

It's important to remember that in spite of these immense changes, one thing stayed the same—filing for Social Security is one of the most important financial decisions you will make in your lifetime, and a financial professional can help ensure you make the right one.

## THE DIVORCE FACTOR

How does a divorced spouse qualify for benefits? If you have gone through a divorce, it might affect the retirement benefit to which you are entitled.

In general, a person can receive benefits as a divorced spouse on a former spouse's Social Security record so long as the following conditions are met:

- the marriage lasted at least 10 years; and
- the person filing for divorce benefits is at least age 62, unmarried, and not entitled to a higher Social Security benefit on his or her own record.*

With all of the different options, strategies and benefits to choose from, you can see why filing for Social Security is more complicated than just mailing in the paperwork. Gathering the data and making yourself aware of all your different options isn't enough to know exactly what to do, however. On the one hand, you can knock yourself out trying to figure out which options are best for you and wondering if you made the best decision. On the other hand, you can work with a financial professional who uses customized software that takes all the variables of your specific situation into account and calculates your best option. You have tens of thousands of different options for filing for your Social Security benefit. If your spouse is a different age than you are, it nearly doubles the amount of options you have. This is far more

---

* *http://www.ssa.gov/retire2/yourdivspouse.htm*

complicated arithmetic than most people can do on their own. If you want a truly accurate understanding of when and how to file, you need someone who will ask you the right questions about your situation, someone who has access to specialized software that can crunch the numbers. The reality is that you need to work with a professional that can provide you with the sophisticated analysis of your situation that will help you make a truly informed decision.

**Important Questions about Your Social Security Benefit:**
- How can I maximize my lifetime benefit? By knowing when and how to file for Social Security. This usually means waiting until you have at least reached your Full Retirement Age. A professional has the experience and the tools to help determine when and how you can maximize your lifetime benefits.
- Who will provide reliable advice for making these decisions? Only a professional has the tools and experience to provide you reliable advice.
- Will the Social Security Administration provide me with the advice? The Social Security Administration cannot provide you with advice or strategies for claiming your benefit. It can give you information about your monthly benefit, but that's it. It also doesn't have the tools to tell you what your specific best option is. It can accurately answer questions about how the system works, but it can't advise you about what decision to make as to how and when to file for benefits.

These specialized software programs are an invaluable resource that can help you understand how and when to file for your Social Security benefit. Not only can they help you better understand all the options available to you—but they can help you understand the financial implications of each choice.

## CHAPTER 6 RECAP //

- To get the most out of your Social Security benefit, you need to file at the right time.
- An investment advisor representative can help you determine when you should file for Social Security to get your Maximum Lifetime Benefit.

# 7

# HOW TO CREATE AN INCOME STREAM WHILE PROTECTING YOUR PRINCIPAL

*What if my Social Security benefit isn't enough?*

The moment that you stop working and start living off the money that you've set aside for retirement can be referred to as the Retirement Cliff. You've worked and earned money your whole life, but the day that you retire, that income comes to an end. That's the day that you have to have other assets that fill the gap. Social Security will fill in some, but you need to come up with something else. After you have calculated your Social Security benefit and have selected the year and month that will maximize your lifetime benefits, it's time to look at your other retirement assets, incomes and options that will reduce or eliminate the drop-off of the Retirement Cliff. You may have a pension, an IRA or Roth IRA, dividends from stock holdings, money from the sale of real estate, rental property, or other sources of income. What other sources of reliable income do you have?

If your monthly Social Security check and your other supplemental income leaves a shortfall in your *desired* income, how are you going to fix it? This shortfall is called the **Income Gap** and it needs to be filled in order to maintain your lifestyle into retirement. If you have a known income gap that you need to fill, you want to know how to fill that income gap with the fewest dollars possible. You basically want to buy that income gap for the least amount of money possible. You don't want it to cost you too much, because you want to get the most out of your other assets, including planning for your future and planning for your legacy. You do that by maximizing your Social Security benefit, leveraging your additional income and looking at other investment tools that can help generate income for you. Your specific needs, of course, should be analyzed by a professional.

## TAKING A HYBRID APPROACH TO YOUR INCOME NEEDS

An investor nearing the time of retirement looks at the assets in their portfolio a little differently than the investor who has another 20 years to accumulate funds. Because this is the money you will be relying on to fill your income gap, you know you need to keep this money safe. However, you also hope to enjoy a nice long retirement, and so you still need to earn some kind of a return. Most people look at their investments in terms of their ability to do either one of two things:

- Provide an opportunity for growth.
- Provide a form of protection or principal guarantees.

But what if there was a way to get the best of both with one option? Insurance companies today have answered the call with new hybrid investment vehicles that can give you a way to get the growth you need along with principal protection.

If you could have the option to contribute more money toward Social Security in order to secure a guaranteed income, it would be a great way to create a Green Money asset that would enhance your retirement. Since that option isn't available, you may seek an investment tool that is similar to Social Security that provides you with a reliable income. It also has the potential to increase the value of your principal investment! This kind of win-win situation exists, and it's called an annuity.

Today, you probably have savings in a variety of assets that you acquired over the years. But you may not have taken time to examine them and assess how they will support your retirement.

It's not about whether the market goes up or down, but when it does. If it goes down at the wrong time for your five or 10 year retirement horizon, you could be in serious danger of losing some of your retirement income.

If you have assets that you would like to structure for retirement income, *an annuity may be the right choice for you.*

**Ask yourself the following questions:**

- How concerned are you about finding a secure financial vehicle to protect your savings?
- How concerned are you that there may be a better way to structure your savings?

If you are concerned about the best way to fill your income gap, an income annuity investment tool is likely a good option for you. Income annuities have many similar qualities to Social Security that give them the same look and feel as that reliable benefit check you get every month. Most importantly, an income annuity can be an efficient and profitable way to solve your income gap.

## WHAT TYPE OF ANNUITY IS RIGHT FOR YOU?

Annuities are popular and reliable investment tools that allow you to secure income during retirement, but the world of annuities can be confusing. The way an annuity gives you income will be different depending on which type of annuity you choose. Some annuities earn returns through direct participation in the market; other annuities give you a fixed rate of return that is guaranteed. There is also a third type of hybrid annuity that gives you the best of both these options.

To help take away the confusion, let's take a look at the three main kinds of annuities on the market today and examine them in terms of how they can fill your income gap. As you shop around for the annuity that best fits your situation, keep in mind that the number one goal when designing a retirement plan is to achieve a balance of both market gains and principal protection.

**Variable Annuities:**

This type of annuity can be thought of as a Red Money investment because it earns returns through direct participation in the stock market. Because this annuity is invested in Hope So mutual funds, your account balance is not guaranteed. A lot of investors get confused by this because in order to give you income, variable annuities are sold with income riders. **It is the purchase of the income rider that gives you some type of guarantee, but a lot of people *think* what they're getting is a guaranteed growth rate on their actual account balance.** They are not. Instead what they are getting is a guarantee that the balance used to calculate their income will be there even if the actual account value drastically falls. Because this is such a confusing subject, we will be talking more about income riders later on in this chapter.

The creation of an income guarantee inside a Red Money investment is what creates a kind of contradiction within the variable annuity, making it one of the most expensive annuities that you can own. Because you are invested in the stock market, you will have to pay fees for the management of the mutual funds in addition to the income rider fees. You will also be assessed a risk fee—sometimes listed as the Mortality & Expense fee—to cover the risk that the insurance company faces when trying to guarantee you an income with a Red Money investment. These fees directly affect any returns that you're able to earn.

If you surrender the annuity, the insurance company will pay you the market value of the asset, regardless of whether it matches, exceeds or falls short of the value at which you bought the contract. If its value has dropped significantly, it might be in your best interest to access your money as an income rather than surrendering your contract. Just like any investment strategy, the amount of risk needs to fit the comfort level of the investor. Annuities are no exception.

**Fixed Annuities:**
For investors who are risk averse, the Green Money guarantees offered by fixed annuities are simple and easy to understand. Just like with your typical bank CD, your rate of return is guaranteed for a fixed period of time. The upside of using a fixed annuity, however, is that you can generally earn a higher return than what you would get with a CD. For example, where a five-year CD might earn you a 1 percent return, a five-year Multi-Year Guaranteed Annuity (MYGA) might earn you 3 percent.

A fixed annuity also works in a way that is very similar to a bank CD. You put your money into an insurance contract where the company guarantees you a set interest rate for set period of time, such as one year or five years or even 10. You will get this guaranteed interest rate regardless of what the stock market does, and you can also find fixed annuities that are set for longer time periods. The danger here is that by locking in a fixed rate, you'll miss out on the opportunity to capture long-term growth. For people who still want to earn some type of respectable return while also keeping their principal safe, a newer hybrid type of annuity might be the right choice.

**Indexed Annuities:**
Indexed annuities give you a taste of market returns combined with the security of a fixed annuity. It achieves this by keeping your money invested in indexed funds. **Indexed funds are linked to the market without being directly exposed to market loss.** You can capture returns that are better than what you would get with a CD or fixed annuity, but without the risk and fees you have to pay with a variable annuity. The way an indexed annuity offsets the risk onto the insurance company is perhaps one of the best features offered by this type of annuity. It works like this:

Every year, the annual reset feature of an indexed annuity credits your returns and locks them in, so they become part of your principal. This is sometimes referred to as ratcheting. If the market gains, you get to capture a portion of those gains; if the market takes a loss, the principal protection feature means you won't lose any money. Your return could be as low as zero, but your account value doesn't fall and you won't lose money due to stock market risk. Because of this, Indexed annuities are considered a Know So, Green Money investment. Guarantees from insurance companies are based on the claims-paying ability of the issuing insurance company. Before choosing which annuity is right for you, be sure to work with a financial professional who can answer questions specific to your situation.

## HOW ANNUITIES FIT INTO AN OVERALL INCOME PLAN

Annuities are popular and reliable investment tools that allow you to secure income during retirement. In its simplest form, an annuity is a way to invest your money that allows you to structure it for income. Annuities come in a variety of modes. Finding the right one for you will take a conversation with your financial professional. Be sure you fully understand the features, benefits and costs of any annuity you are considering before investing money.

**Here is how they can work:**

When you put your money into an annuity, you are essentially buying an investment product from an insurance company. It is a contract between you and the insurance company that provides the investment tool. Let's say you have saved $100,000 and need it to generate income to meet your needs above and beyond your Social Security and pension checks. You give the $100,000 to an insurance company, who in turn invests it to generate growth.

They usually select investments that have modest returns over long term horizons. In other words, they generally put it somewhere stable and predictable. Most commonly, they will invest it in a combination of bonds and treasuries that are safer and dependable ways to grow money. They use the money from the insurance products they sell to invest, use a portion of the returns to generate profits for themselves, and return a portion to clients in the form of payouts, claims, and structured income options.

The annual reset feature of the indexed annuity means that if the market goes down, you don't suffer a loss. Instead, the insurance company absorbs it. But if the market goes up, you share with the insurance company some of the profit made on the gain. The amount of gain you get is called your annuity participation rate. Typically the insurer will cap the amount of gain you can realize at somewhere between 3 and 7 percent. If the market goes up 10 percent, you would realize a portion of that gain (whatever percentage you are capped at). This means you to never lose money on your investment, while always gaining a portion of the upswings. The measurement period of your annuity can be calculated monthly, weekly and even daily, but most annuities are measured annually. The level of the index when you buy and the index level one year later will determine the amount of loss or gain. You and the insurance company are betting that the market will generally go up over time.

## CONSUMER ALERT: HOW AN INCOME RIDER REALLY WORKS

Income riders are often sold with annuities as a way to address the fear of running out of money. In most cases they guarantee that should your account value fall below zero, your income payments will still continue. That can be a nice guarantee to have, and the peace of mind is often worth the 1 percent fee, however, many people are sold riders who don't really need them. Income rider fees can add up to thousands of dollars during the lifetime of the rider, so this is one feature you don't want to pay for if you don't need it. Income riders go by many different names depending on the type of annuity and the insurance company that is offering them, and their benefits and features aren't always understood. We'd like to take the time to explain how they work here.

When you use that $100,000 to buy a contract with an insurance company in the form of an annuity, you are pegging your money on an index. It could be the S&P 500, the Dow Jones Industrial Average or any number of indexes. We talked earlier about how the power of annual reset means that when the market goes up, you get to capture a portion of those returns; when the market goes down, your principal is safe and the worse you can do is earn a zero return.

To generate income from the indexed annuity, you select something called an income rider. Essentially, the purchase of the rider creates a separate account that the insurance company uses to calculate your income payment. We'll call this account the Income Account, although it goes by different names depending on the insurance company. As the insurance company holds your money and invests it, they generate a return on it that they use to pay you a regular monthly income based on the higher number of the Income Account created by the purchase of the rider. The insurance company has to outperform the amount that they pay you in order to make a profit.

Your Income Account is a larger number than what your investment is actually worth, and if you select the income rider, it will increase in value over time, providing you with more income guaranteed to last the rest of your life. **However, consumers need to beware this one important distinction: you do NOT have access to the money in your Income Account as a lump sum.** This is an annuitized stream of money, and so the only way to get to this money is by taking it as an income. You can only cash out the funds of your actual account, which we'll call your Account Value. With a variable annuity, it is your Account Value that fluctuates with the market; with the fixed and indexed annuity, your Account Value has principal guarantees.

Remember, insurance companies make long-term investments that provide them with predictable flows of money. They like to stabilize the amount of money that goes in and out of their doors instead of paying and receiving large unpredictable chunks at once. When you opt for an income rider, an insurance company can reliably predict how much money they will pay out to you over a set period of time. It's predictable, and they like that. They can base their business on those predictable numbers.

Is an income rider right for your situation? They do offer certain benefits that can be helpful for the retiree who is worried about running out of money, but you don't have to purchase an income rider in order to generate income payments from an annuity. Talk to a qualified financial professional to find out if an income rider is right for you.

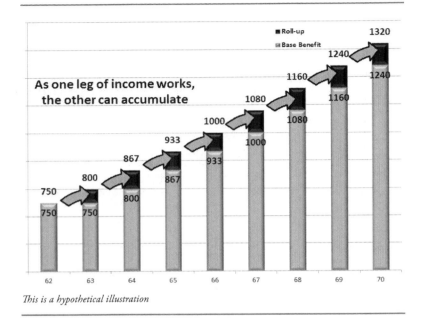

*This is a hypothetical illustration*

## WHY IS THERE A SURRENDER CHARGE?

In order to encourage investors to leave their money in their annuity contracts, insurance companies create surrender periods that protect their investments. If you remove your money from the annuity contract during the surrender period, you will pay a penalty and will not be able to receive your entire investment amount back. A typical surrender period is 10 years. If after three years you decide that you want your $100,000 back, the insurance company has that money tied up in bonds and other investments with the understanding that they will have it for another seven years. Because they will take a hit on removing the money from their investments prematurely, you will have to pay a surrender charge that makes up for their loss. During the surrender period, an annuity is not a demand deposit account like a savings or checking account. The higher returns that you are guaranteed from an annuity are dependent on the timeframe you selected. The longer an insurance company can hold your money, the easier it is for them to guarantee a predictable return on it.

If you leave your money in the annuity contract, you get a reliable monthly income no matter what happens in the market. Once the surrender period has expired, you can remove your money whenever you want. Your money becomes liquid again because the insurance company has used it in an investment that fit the timeline of your surrender period. For many people, this is an attractive trade off that can provide a creative solution for filling their income gap.

## WHEN IS AN ANNUITY WITH AN INCOME RIDER RIGHT FOR YOU?

A good financial professional can help you make that determination by taking the time to listen closely to your situation and understanding what your needs are as you enter retirement. Every salesperson has a bag full of brochures and PowerPoint presentations, but they need to know exactly what the financial concerns of their individual clients are in order to help them make the most informed and beneficial decision. Some people need income today; others need it in five or 10 years. Others may have their income needs met but are planning to move closer to their children and will need to buy a house in 10 years. Or, if you want income in 15 years, you might want to choose a different investment product for 10 years, and then switch to an annuity with an income rider during the last five years of your timeline.

If you have an amount of money set aside that you want to protect and grow but that you don't need for income, a different kind of rider might be appropriate for you.

## HOW TO PROTECT AND GROW YOUR MONEY FOR LATER

If you have an amount of money that you know you want to leave for your loved ones, then you'll want to figure out how to best position these funds for growth and safety. You might also want to know that you can access this money if you need to. While annuities are a long-term investment, adding a rider gives you more flexibility. There is another kind of rider on the market that is designed to help you grow the money that you want to use later, either as a legacy for your heirs or as a way to help plan for your spouse's continuing income. This kind of rider is known as a death benefit rider.

A death benefit rider functions in a way that is similar to an income rider. It creates a second account that grows at an accelerated and guaranteed rate—sometimes as high as 7 percent—for a fee that is usually 1 percent or lower. It is the second account, which we'll call the Death Benefit Account, which goes to your heirs in the event of your passing. As with the Income Account, you cannot access the money in the Death Benefit Account as a lump sum, because this money is set in growth-mode for the long-term. You can access your regular account—the Account Value—and most insurance companies allow you to access up to 10 percent without penalty.

Sometimes these hybrid annuities are sold with bonus money. When you purchase a death benefit rider, the bonus money is automatically credited to BOTH your actual Account Value and your Death Benefit Account. Different insurance companies offer different bonus amounts and contract terms, but they are based on your age at the time you sign the contract. For example, if you select an indexed annuity with a death benefit rider and a bonus of 8 percent, and your initial deposit into the contract is $200,000, then your Account Value balance would be $216,000, and your Death Benefit Account value would be $216,000.

Now, just like with an income rider, the money in your Death Benefit Account grows at a higher, guaranteed rate than the money in your regular account. For example, if the market dropped by 30 percent this year, your Account Value would stay the same at $216,000, but your Death Benefit Account would still grow at the guaranteed rate, which in this case we'll say is 4 percent. The balance of your Death Benefit Account is now $224,640. The following year, the market performs like gangbusters and the index earns a nice fat 10 percent. Now your actual Account Value is $237,600, but your Death Benefit Account grows by 10 percent PLUS the 4 percent guaranteed, for a total gain of 14 percent. Your Death Benefit Account is now sitting at $256,089.

As the name suggests, the money in the Death Benefit Account is only transferred to your heirs upon your death. Using an indexed annuity with a rider like this can be a great way to grow money for future income. When one spouse passes away, all of the funds in the accelerated growth account are passed to the surviving spouse to be used for income or whatever they wish. They will have full access to the money as a lump sum, or they can roll it into another annuity to create their own income stream.

## SINGLE PREMIUM IMMEDIATE ANNUITIES (SPIA)

A single premium immediate annuity is simply a contract between you and an insurance company. SPIAs are structured so that you pay a lump sum of money (a single premium) to an insurance company, and they give you a guaranteed income over an agreed upon time period. That time period could be five years, or it could be for the remainder of your lifetime. Guarantees from insurance companies are based on the claims-paying ability of the issuing insurance company.

SPIAs provide investors with a stream of reliable income when they can't afford to take the risk of losing money in a fluctuating market. While there is general faith that the market always trends up, at least in the long-term, if you are focusing on income over a shorter period of time, you may not be able to take a big hit in the market. Beyond normal market volatility, interest rates also come with an inherent level of uncertainty, making it hard to create a dependable income on your own. SPIAs reduce risk for you by giving you regular monthly, quarterly or yearly payments that can begin the moment you buy the contract. Your financial professional can walk you through a series of different payment options to help you select the one that most closely fits your needs.

**Quick Annuity Reminders:**
- Some contracts will allow you to draw income from the high water mark that the market reaches each year. The income rider will then begin calculating its value from the high water mark.
- Income annuities are investment tools that look and feel a bit like Social Security. Every year you allow the money to grow with the market, and it will "roll up" by a specific amount, paying out a specific percent to you as income each year.
- Annuities can work very well to create income, and a financial professional can help you find the one that best matches your income need, and can also structure it to work perfectly for you.

**Managing Risk Within Your Annuity:**
Just like any investment strategy, the amount of risk needs to fit the comfort level of the investor. Annuities are no exception. Without going into too much detail, here are some additional ways to manage risk with annuity options:
- If you want to structure an annuity investment for growth over a long period of time, you can select a variable annuity. The value of your principal investment follows the

market and can lose or gain value with the market. This type of annuity can also have an income rider, but it is really more useful as an accumulation tool that bets on an improving market. A 40-year-old couple, for example, will probably want to structure more for growth and take on more risk than someone in their 70s. The 40-year-old couple may select a variable annuity with an income rider that kicks in when they plan to retire. If it rises with the market or outperforms it, the value of their investment has grown. If the market loses ground over the duration of the contract or their annuity underperforms, they can still rely on the income rider.

- If you are 68 years old and you have more immediate income needs that you need to come up with above and beyond your Social Security, you need a low risk, reliable source of income. If you choose an annuity option, you are looking for something that will pay out an income right away over a relatively short timeframe. You probably want to opt for a SPIA that pays you immediately and spans a five year period, as well as an additional annuity that begins paying you in five years, and another longer term annuity that begins paying you in 10 years. Bear in mind that each annuity contract has its own costs and fees. Review these with your financial professional before you determine the best products and strategies for your situation.

The following example shows just how helpful an indexed annuity option can be for a retiree:

» *Lyndon and Carol are 62 years old and have decided to run the numbers to see what their retirement is going to look like. They know they currently need $6,000 per month to pay their* *bills and maintain their current lifestyle. They have also done their Social Security homework and have determined that, between the two of them, they will receive $4,200 per month in benefits. They also receive $350 per month in rent from a tenant who lives in a small carriage house in their backyard. Between their Social Security and the monthly rent income, they will be short $1,450 per month.*

*They do have an additional asset, however. They have been contributing for years to an IRA that has reached a value of $350,000. They realize that they have to figure out how to turn the $350,000 in their IRA into $1,450 per month for the rest of their life. At first glance, it may seem like they will have plenty of money. With some quick calculations, they find they have 240 months, or nearly 20 years, of monthly income before they exhaust the account. When you consider income tax, the potential for higher taxes in the future, and market fluctuations (because many IRAs are invested in the market), the amount in the IRA seems to have a little less clout. Every dollar Lyndon and Carol take out of the IRA is subject to income tax, and if they leave the remainder in the IRA, they run the risk of losing money in a volatile market. Once they retire and stop getting a paycheck every two weeks, they also stop contributing to their IRA. And when they aren't supplementing its growth with their own money, they are entirely dependent on market growth. That's a scary prospect. They could also withdraw the money from the IRA and put it in a savings account or CD, but removing all the money at once will put them in a tax bracket that will claim a huge portion of the value of the IRA. A seemingly straightforward asset has now become a complicated equation. Lyndon and Carol didn't know what to do, so they met with their financial professional.*

*Their financial professional suggested that they use the money to purchase an indexed annuity with an income rider. They selected an annuity that was designed for their specific situation. They took the lump sum from their IRA, placed it in an indexed annuity taking advantage of annual reset so they never lost the value of their investment. In return, they were guaranteed the $1,450 of income per month that they needed to meet their retirement goals. The simplicity of the contract allowed them to do an analysis with their professional just once to understand the product. They basically put their money in an investment crockpot where they didn't have to look at it or manage it. They just needed to let it simmer. In fact, their professional was able to find an annuity for them that allowed them their $1,450 monthly payment with a lump sum of $249,455, leaving them more than $100,000 to reinvest somewhere else. Keep in mind that annuities are tax deferred, meaning you will pay tax on the income you receive from an annuity in the year you receive it.*

*» Tina is 60 years old and is wondering how she can use her assets to provide her with a retirement income. She has a $5,000 per month income need. If she starts withdrawing her Social Security benefit in six years at age 66, it will provide her with $2,200 per month. She also has a pension that kicks in at age 70 that will give her another $1,320 per month.*

*That leaves an income gap of $2,800 from ages 66 to 69, and then an income gap of $1,480 at age 70 and beyond. If Tina uses only Green Money to solve her income need, she will need to deposit $918,360 at 2 percent interest to meet her monthly goal for her lifetime. If she opts to use Red Money and withdraws the amount she needs each month from the market, let's say the S & P 500, she will run out of cash in 10 years if she invested between the years of 2000 and 2012.*

*Suffering a market downturn like that during the period for which she is relying on it for retirement income will change her life, and not for the better.*

*Working with a financial professional to find a better way, Tina found that she could take a hybrid approach to fill her income gap. Her professional recommended two different income vehicles: one that allowed her to deposit just $190,161 with a 2 percent return, and one that was a $146,000 income annuity. These tools filled her income gap with $336,161, requiring her to spend $582,000 less money to accomplish her goal! Working with a professional to find the right tools for her retirement needs saved Tina over half a million dollars.*

## CREATING AN INCOME PLAN

Creating an income plan before you retire allows you to satisfy your need for lifetime income and ensures that your lifestyle can last as long as you do. You also want to create a plan that operates in the most efficient way possible. Doing so will give more security to your Need Later Money and will potentially allow you to build your legacy down the road.

Here is a basic roadmap of what we have covered so far:

- Review your income needs and look specifically at the shortfall you may have during each year of your retirement based on your Social Security income, and income from any other assets you have.
- Ask yourself where you are in your distribution phase. Is retirement one year away? 10 years away? Last year?
- Determine how much money you need and how you need to structure your existing assets to provide for that need.
- If you have an asset from which you need to generate income, consider options offered by purchasing an income rider on an annuity.

## CHAPTER 7 RECAP //

- The number one goal of any comprehensive retirement plan is to eliminate risk while capturing some upside gains of the market. Today's income annuities offer retirees a hybrid investment option that can accomplish both goals.

- Although an annuity is an income-producing asset that does not subject your income to market risk, it still has the opportunity to grow. Indexed annuities participate in linked market growth without market loss through a strategy known as indexing. Indexing combined with the power of annual reset gives you both growth and safety of your principal.

- An income rider can be purchased for a fee to create a separate account that grows at a higher rate than the actual account value. Be aware that this second account cannot be accessed as a lump sum and may not be what you need.

- If your main objective is to grow and protect your money for later, a death benefit may be a more suitable rider. It functions much like an income rider in that it creates a second account that grows or rolls up at a higher rate. This second account cannot be accessed as a lump sum during your lifetime but it does increase the potential death benefit for your beneficiaries.

- Be sure you understand the features, benefits, costs and fees associated with any annuity product before you invest.

# 8

# WAKE UP TO THE REALITIES:
## CATASTROPHIC ILLNESS AND HOW
## TO PROTECT YOURSELF

Building a house is a major undertaking. This is the structure that will shelter and protect you and your loved ones for the next several years, possibly even decades. As such you want to set a good foundation and use the best quality materials that you can. You also want to work with someone who knows how to get you the highest quality supplies for the money, someone who builds in a way that protects you from the risks. Nobody wants to work with a hasty builder who can't wait to get the job done so they can move onto other things. The same kind of thing can be said of building a retirement plan.

The process of turning a portfolio into an income source that can support all your needs for the next 20 to 30 years is a surprisingly complicated task. Because of the added years medical science has gifted us, most of us are going to see numerous changes—in the stock market, in our government, and in the world. One major change that a lot of people over look are the changes that happen as we age.

This is a difficult subject to bring up, but as professionals who have seen and experienced the worst, we want more than anything for you to be prepared. Everyone thinks that catastrophic events won't happen to them. Until they do. We are writing this difficult chapter so that you don't have to live through the nightmare like we did. It is possible to take relatively small actions now to protect yourself against catastrophic events that might come up later. Consider the following story based on a real-life scenario.

> » *Jerry and Diane were diligent savers. They set aside money every month for retirement even when it wasn't easy to do. They clipped coupons, bought used vehicles, and stayed in the same house for over 30 years until it was paid off. Jerry and Diane also never took vacations because they figured that when they retired, they would enjoy the ultimate vacation: Hawaii. It was their dream to take a month-long trip to the island of paradise. They would view stunning waterfalls, take a helicopter ride over the cliffs of Waimea Canyon, snorkel the submerged volcanic crater of Molokini, and swim the seven sacred pools. They would send postcards to all their relatives and friends, go to luaus, learn to hula, and then come home and enjoy those memories together for the rest of their lives. That was all they wanted: one big trip to Hawaii. The rest of their money they would leave to their kids.*
>
> *When they retired, Jerry and Diane had $500,000 in their portfolio and they were proud of what they'd saved. Di-*

ane started pricing package deals to Hawaii. She researched the islands and learned about the best places to stay. A year into their retirement, Diane asked her husband,

"Can I start planning our trip and booking our tours?"

Jerry was watching the stock market. Things were uncertain and he was worried about their oil stocks. He also knew they had to get a few repairs done around the house.

"We'd better wait a few months," he said. "Let things settle down."

A few months went by and Jerry didn't feel any better about things. He had a new list of worries, one of them being the vision in his right eye. It started as a blind spot and then things started to get fuzzy. One year later, Jerry was declared legally blind because of diabetes.

Unable to drive himself or go where he wanted to go, Jerry's mood started to tank. He often threw things across the room that he bumped into, sometimes injuring himself. One day when he was home alone, Jerry got dizzy, fell, and fractured his hip. Diane talked with his doctor and they hired an in-home health care aid to help with his daily activities of living. This cost them $50,336 a year where they lived in Chicago, but it seemed to help for a while. *Jerry was able to stay home in his own surroundings, and they did this for three years.

When Jerry hit age 70, complications from his diabetes continued to worsen and memory issues started to develop. Jerry got easily confused and often argued with the nurse about which medication he had taken. He also sometimes got up in the middle of the night because he thought it was time to start his day. Diane worried about what would happen if he took another fall, and so under the recommendation of

---

*Jerry's doctor, they moved him to a 24-hour facility where he could receive round the clock care. Diane did her research and found a nursing him that had a good reputation for patient care in the metro area, but it came with a price tag of $94,896 a year.*

*"What are you going to do?" a friend asked Diane.*

*"Well I'm going to take care of my Jerry," she said. And she did. Diane spent all of the money they had in their savings, every dollar they had put away for their big trip to Hawaii was spent on health care for her Jerry, but what else could she do?*

*Diane visited him every day. And Jerry told her that he still wanted her to go to Hawaii when he was gone.*

*"At least one of us should see it," he said.*

*Jerry had no idea that all of their money was gone. They were now on Medicaid and all Diane had to live on were their two Social Security checks. She couldn't have more than a certain amount of money in the bank, was limited as to which assets she could own, and there would be no money left for the kids. But Diane didn't want Jerry to know this.*

*"I will go to Hawaii," she told him. "I'm planning my trip now."*

*Every day she told him about all of the things she would see and do in Hawaii. Every day, she sat with him and talked to him so that her Jerry could go there in his imagination, because that is the only trip that they would ever get to take.*

## THIS IS WHY YOU NEED TO PLAN

Most people understand the kind of financial loss that can happen in the event of a stock market downturn, but they don't realize

---

*\* http://newsroom.genworth.com/2016-06-28-Genworth-2016-Annual-Cost-of-Care-Study-Home-Care-Costs-Increased-in-Illinois-Overall-Costs-are-Up*

that a catastrophic illness can have the same kind of debilitating effect. Chronic illness tends to be a gradual condition that gets worse over time, so the money slowly trickles away. Most people don't want to think about something like this happening to them or their loved ones, and so they don't prepare. We take a different approach: think about it once and make a plan, then you don't have to worry about it ever again.

Long-term care is one area where people have a lot of misperceptions. They think, "that will never happen to me," or they mistakenly assume that they can't afford to prepare. Had Jerry and Diane known they had options, they could have worked with a dedicated financial professional to put a plan in place. They could have left money to their kids and gone to Hawaii instead of worrying about market timing. They could have done so much more with what they had if only they'd known what to do.

**There is almost always something that you can do.**

If you, like Jerry and Diane, have worked hard and saved your money, then you have two choices about the type of long-term care planning that you can do:

**Catastrophic Planning**: This is basically the kind of planning that Jerry and Diane did. They took a wait and see approach, and then dealt with the situation as best they could once it came up. Had they sought the advice of a financial professional or independent firm that specializes in this kind of thing right after Jerry's diagnosis, they could have potentially done *some* planning to protect more of their assets. Our firm works with an eldercare attorney who specializes in the legal issues of Medicaid planning. While the cost of catastrophic planning is higher than pre-planning, it's usually better to at least do something rather than nothing once you find yourself in a long-term care situation. Of course, had they done their planning before disaster hit, they would have been able to realize more of their retirement dreams.

**Pre-planning:** With this kind of planning, you address all of the risks before anything bad happens. Jerry and Diane did the hard work of saving for their retirement; there was no reason they couldn't have afforded their dream trip to Hawaii. Where they made a mistake was not getting together a comprehensive plan. Not only could we have put together a plan that would have guaranteed their income and given them a growth plan for their Need Later Money, they could have travelled while Jerry was still healthy enough to enjoy it. There are also insurance solutions available today that can give you asset-based protection that can leverage your money, so that for every dollar you put into the policy, you get two or three back to spend on long-term care. There are also policies and products that offer long-term care riders and death benefits. Had Jerry and Diane gotten a simple life insurance policy with long-term care benefits, they could have protected the money for their children and ensured continuation of income for Diane. Even though Jerry's condition was far worse than Diane could have imagined, just taking this simple step could have protected up to 50 percent of their assets.

We share this story with you to remind you that you that you have more options than you think. What follows is a basic primer of what you need to know about long-term care planning.

## LONG-TERM CARE 101

Anyone can put their investments on auto-pilot, sit back, and watch the annual distribution checks come in. Putting together a comprehensive plan is another thing entirely. It's kind of like solving a Rubix Cube puzzle. Every time you move something of one color, something of another color changes. The easy way is to just take off all the stickers and redo the sides until all the colors are same. The problem with that is, after a few years, the stickers fall off. We don't do planning that way.

We take long-term care planning and break it down into two phases:

**Phase one** is completed when we put together the income plan and it asks the question, "How will you fund long-term care?"

**Phase two** is completed when we do your legacy planning and it answers the questions, "How can we best protect your assets using Medicaid strategies?"

We divide long-term care planning into two parts to help you face the reality that during retirement, either one of two things will happen:

- Either you will get sick and pass away
  OR
- You will pass away without getting sick.

When you have a plan, you know you'll be fine either way.

## Who has your back?

The first step of Phase One doesn't cost you anything; it's simply an investment of your time. Get together with your spouse, and talk about what you want to see happen. Get together with your kids, and make sure you communicate your preferences so that everybody is on the same page. Oftentimes, it's the kids who feel responsible for their parents, and they worry about salespeople who might prey on their fears. A lot of people think that long-term care planning means buying an expensive long-term care policy. This isn't the case at all. Most long-term care is not medical care, but rather assistance with the basic personal tasks of everyday life, sometimes called Activities of Daily Living (ADLs). Most people also prefer to receive care in the comfort of their own home, which means you want a plan that can accommodate your preferences.

**What is long-term care?**

There is a wide range of services that all fall under the category of long-term care. Everything from taking out the garbage to dialysis treatment could be part of a home-care service, and on-site facilities now range from adult day-care services, assisted living facilities, and full time nursing homes. As we age it gets more difficult to do ordinary tasks such as making the bed, grocery shopping, or walking the dog. You can think of the services offered in the areas as being in one of two categories: health services or homemaker services.

**Home Health Aide Services** are concerned with medical needs and they include services such as:

- Skilled nursing care
- Therapies: Occupational, speech, and physical
- Dietary management by registered dietician
- Management of prescription medication
- Durable medical equipment
- Case management
- Personal care
- Caregiver training
- Health promotion and disease prevention
- Hospice care

**Homemaker Services** support the activities of daily living and include services such as:

- Meal preparations or delivery
- Personal care (dressing, bathing, eating, transferring to or from a bed or chair, etc.)
- Transportation
- Shopping
- Home repairs and modifications
- Home safety assessments

- Homemaker and chore services

**How much does it cost?**
The cost of care varies from state-to-state according to the services required. In the state of Illinois, for example, you can expect to pay an average of $132 a day for homemaker services and $138 a day for a home health aide according to Genworth's 2016 numbers. * The cost for a private room in a nursing home averages $184 a day for a semi-private room and $205 a day for a private room. What's interesting is that Genworth predicts the cost of this care to be $332 a day and $370 a day respectively 20 years from now.** The inflation rate for healthcare in the United States was at 5.8 percent in 2015—more than double the U.S. inflation rate.*** How much will long-term care cost when you need it?

**How can we pay for it?**
You basically have four options when it comes to paying for long-term care:

1. Pay out of pocket: With this option, you take a portion of your assets not needed for income and set it aside for your long-term care. When the time comes and either you or your spouse require accelerated health care, you know what funds to tap into.

2. Traditional long-term care insurance: This option becomes more expensive and difficult to qualify the older you get. You essentially transfer the risk of your long-term care expenses onto an insurance company. In exchange for knowing you have contracted protection in place, you

---

* *https://www.genworth.com/about-us/industry-expertise/cost-of-care.html*
** *https://www.genworth.com/about-us/industry-expertise/cost-of-care.html*
*** *http://www.zetemaproject.org/about*

pay out a premium like you do with your car insurance. If you never have a long-term care event, then all the money you paid in to the policy reverts back to the insurance company.

3. Aid and Attendance: Aid and Attendance (A&A) is a little-known benefit funded by Congress for qualifying wartime veterans and their surviving spouses. If you or your spouse served in the military, then you may be eligible for this benefit designed to help when paying out-of-pocket for long-term care expenses.

4. Using Life Insurance: More and more life insurance companies are offering alternatives to traditional policies that have both living benefits and death benefits built-in. Life insurance companies sometimes call long-term care benefits *living benefits* because you don't have to die in order to receive the money. The plan provides you with the means to pay for home health care or a nursing home facility while you are alive, in addition to a death benefit protection that can go to your spouse or family in the event that you never need to spend the living benefits. Other options include critical care riders available on indexed annuities. These solutions are easier to qualify for and require no health exam and no underwriting as long as you can perform all six of the ADLs.

## HOW TO PREPARE FOR THE UNEXPECTED

Financial planning is about more than protecting your money from stock market risk; it's also about preparing for those unexpected "what if" life scenarios.

- If you get sick
- If you die
- If you don't get sick

A lot of people avoid planning for the "what if I get sick" scenario because with traditional long-term care insurance, if you don't have a qualifying event, then all the money you paid into the policy reverts back to the insurance company. If you've done the saving and have the funds to plan for this, you might take advantage of today's newer life insurance solutions. One of the best out there is something you might call a life and long term care combo plan. The cost for the living benefits offered by these types of plans is comparable to the cost of traditional long-term care insurance and the policies are funded by monthly payments. You can also choose to fund the policy through a lump-sum payment, which can be a smart place to put the money you have been earning dismal returns in bank CDs. Unlike traditional policies, the money is NOT lost if there is no need for long-term care because the policy also provides your loved ones with a death benefit. While cost can sometimes be an issue, when you consider the multiple benefits and flexibility offered, many people find this option to give them the best of both worlds. It covers your back in each of these three scenarios:.

- **If you get sick:** This type of policy offers living benefits that kick in should you need home health aid or homemaker services. They can also assist with your nursing home expenses. It's usually the inability to perform two out of the six ADLs that trigger the event, and you're able to receive a much greater benefit than you would have had you relied on out-of-pocket funds alone. For example, Jerry and Diane could have purchased $400,000 worth of coverage for just $100,000 of their savings.

- **If you die:** As you might expect, life insurance is at its best when used to provide for your loved ones in the event of your passing. The death benefits for these types of policies are once again able to leverage your money so you can do more with every dollar you invest; best of all, the benefits are paid to your family tax-free. Using our earlier example, Jerry and Diane could have purchased a $200,000 death benefit for that same $100,000.

- **If you _don't_ get sick:** The nice thing about these combo plans is that they give you access to your money. Jerry and Diane could have put $100,000 into one of these policies, and then used this money to go on their dream trip to Hawaii. With just a little bit of forethought, they could have accomplished all their goals—increased the money they left to their family and gone to Hawaii—all while also planning for their long-term care.

As mentioned earlier, there are two ways you can fund this combination plan: either with a lump sum or with monthly payments. If you choose the monthly payment options, then you do not have the immediate access to liquidity, however your money is still leveraged. The minute the contract goes into effect, you can have the peace of mind knowing that whether you get sick and die or just plain die, you, your family, and loved ones are protected.

## HOW TO PROTECT YOUR ASS(ETS)

Making sure that you and your spouse are covered in the event of a catastrophic illness is the right thing to do, but it's only the first step. In many cases, your expenses might continue farther into the future than you would like. This was the case for Ma Dowling. She endured 22 years in a nursing home facility. Forty percent of all individuals age 65 and older will enter into a nursing home with an average stay of 2.44 years, and 10 percent will need care for five years or more.*

You may find yourself a candidate for Medicaid if you burn through all of your assets. Should you someday find yourself

---

* _http://news.morningstar.com/articlenet/article.aspx?id=564139_

in this situation, there are a few things to be aware of that may improve your outcome.

First and foremost, the state becomes the contingent beneficiary of your assets once you go on Medicaid. Your home is protected as long as one spouse is still alive, but once that spouse dies, the state becomes the beneficiary of all your assets except for income, and there are limits on the amount of income you can have. There are strict rules from the 2012 Deficit Reduction Act from the State of Illinois surrounding the assets and income that you are allowed to keep if you or your spouse enter into a nursing home and need Medicaid assistance. These rules vary from state to state, but in Illinois for 2016, they were as follows:

- **Community Spouse Resource Allowance:** You can keep no more than $109,560 in investments such as bank CDs and mutual funds if your spouse is in a nursing home.
- **Community Spouse Maintenance Needs Allowance:** Income is limited to $2,739 a month and your bank savings is limited to $2,000 in the State of Illinois. Rules vary by state.
- **Personal Needs Allowance:** As a single applicant in a nursing home, you can keep up to $2,000 in the bank and $30 a month for income.*

**You may be able to avoid having to put down all of your assets if you plan for this event ahead of time.** When you apply for Medicaid, they have a 60-month look-back policy which means they will ask if you have transferred or moved any of your assets in the last five years. If you answer, "No," to this question, then you may qualify for aid.

Phase one of the plan is to purchase long-term care protection, while phase two involves proper planning using *a correct trust.* A

---

* *https://www.dhs.state.il.us/page.aspx?item=61574*

Family Trust or Medicaid Trust can serve as protector to a portion of your assets because with these legal documents, your home and assets are not listed in your name. You can still maintain control over these assets (and you may continue living in your home), but you get to choose your family members or loved ones as your contingent beneficiary instead of the state.

**Are there any assets you have that you would like to protect and keep?**

- Pass book savings
- Checking accounts
- Certificates of deposit
- Stocks and bonds
- Mutual funds
- Government savings bonds
- IRAs not under distribution
- Deferred annuities that are not Medicaid structured
- Real estate investments
- Vacation home

Consumer Alert: not all financial professionals know how to properly build a comprehensive plan that protects both your health and your assets. We have seen paperwork that's been completed improperly and we've seen situations where not all the "I's" were dotted and not all the "T's" crossed, resulting in a plan that was full of holes.

If you take the time to do this planning, make sure you find a qualified professional who is up-to-date with current legislation and rules. Most states have a *partnership program*. These programs dictate that for every dollar you have in long-term care protection, you can keep that dollar in assets. That would help residents of Illinois because qualified money in an IRA is hard to protect. The bottom line is this: act before it's too late. If you want to protect your assets from Medicaid spenddown, then talk to a qualified financial professional who works with an attorney who specializes in Elder Care law and an expert in Medicaid strategies.

The goal with the asset protection plan is to properly position your assets so that if you qualify for Medicaid, you do so without losing everything that you own. This can be achieved by setting up a special trust and then paying out-of-pocket, using long-term care insurance, or applying Aid and Attendance for the first five years of an illness or catastrophic event. That way, if the event goes on longer than anyone ever expected, you're covered. If the event passes, you're still covered. Either way, if you take care of Phase One and Phase Two of this critical planning, you'll have the peace of mind that comes from knowing you can achieve all your retirement goals while also maintaining your dignity and independence all the days of your life.

## A HOUSE OF STRAW OR A HOUSE OF BRICKS: YOU CHOOSE

There are a lot of financial professionals in the industry who neglect to bring up the subject of long-term care planning. We don't blame them—it's not an easy thing to talk about. Ultimately, the burden of this responsibility lies with you. Will you choose to build a house of straw or a house of bricks? Even if you think it won't happen to you, even if you are a decidedly cheerful and optimistic person, life is full of surprises for us all. If you have done a good job of saving for retirement, you owe it to yourself, your spouse, and your loved ones to protect this money to the best of your ability.

The reality is that either one of two things will happen: you will either get sick or then pass away, or you will simply pass away without getting sick. It used to be that life insurance products that helped with long-term care only addressed option number one. Today, you can address both outcomes. With the living benefits offered by today's life insurance products, you can build a house of bricks. The big bad wolf of long-term care can huff and puff and blow all he wants; with a proper plan in place, your house and your retirement dreams will stand strong.

## CHAPTER 8 RECAP //

- Planning for long-term care is one way to add a layer of protection to your retirement savings. The average duration for long-term care services is three years, but 20 percent of people who need long-term care will require services for 5 or more years.*
- Traditional long-term care insurance can be expensive and if it is not used, the money paid into the policy is lost. With life insurance solutions, the money is not lost should the policyholder never need care. If you get sick, you are protected. If you don't get sick, you have greater access to funds and the money is passed along to your named beneficiaries.
- With proper planning and the establishment of the correct kind of trust, it is possible to protect your assets from Medicaid spend-down. Seek counsel from an attorney who specializes in
- Elder Care Law and look for a financial professional knowledgeable in the area of legacy planning and is up to date with current rules for estate transfer and long-term care planning in your state.

---

* *http://longtermcare.gov/the-basics/*

# 9
# ACCUMULATION

Understanding your Social Security benefit, filling the income gap and making an overall plan that meets your retirement income needs is no small task. Once you have worked with a financial professional to structure your income needs, it's time to take a look at the future. With your immediate income needs met, you have the opportunity to take your additional assets and leverage them for profit to supplement your income in the future, to prepare for anticipated health care costs or to contribute to your legacy. Stable income also means that you should have the staying power to stick with your investment portfolio through the ups and downs in the market.

## MATH OF REBOUNDS

A fickle market can raise the eyebrows of even the most veteran investor. Taking a hit in the market hurts no matter how stable your income. Part of the pain comes from knowing that when you take a step back in the market, it requires an even larger step forward to return to where you were. As the market goes up and down, those larger gains you need to realize to get back to zero start to look even more daunting.

Consider this: if the market experienced a downturn and your investment lost 30 percent of its value, then your investment would need to grow by 43 percent the following year just to make up for the previous year's loss. The unfortunate truth of the matter is that it's not always an easy task for an investment to rebound from a loss—and it may not rebound the year following the loss. More often than not, it just takes time.

The order in which an investment's returns are realized can have an incredible impact on its value. This concept is referred to as the sequence of returns of an investment. To understand just how powerful this concept is, imagine you have two portfolios that you are withdrawing the same amount of income from and have yielded the same returns. After 25 years, these two portfolios should have the same ending value, right?

Wrong. If you're taking income from the accounts, then the sequence in which they realize their returns will matter greatly. For example, imagine portfolio B started off strong and then the market suffered a downswing. It would still be doing quite well because its early growth would have insulated it enough to be able to absorb the hit.

Portfolio A, on the other hand, could experience the exact same rates of return but just in the opposite order. Portfolio A would not be doing as well because the steady withdrawals would make it impossible for the portfolio to recover from the huge loss it suffered right out of the gate. Ultimately, if you're taking income from an account, then the order in which it realizes its returns can have a dramatic impact on your bottom line.

Understanding the concept of sequence of returns can also help you avoid falling prey to the "Flaw of Averages," which refers to the idea that relying on an investment's average rate of return as a primary indicator of its performance can be problematic. Think of it this way: if you wanted to cross a river and you knew that its average depth was four feet, would you deem it safe to cross?

Hopefully not. Just because a river has an average depth of four feet that doesn't mean it will be four feet deep the whole way across: it could very well be two feet deep everywhere except for a 12-foot drop off in the middle. Although the river would still have an average depth of four feet, crossing it might not necessarily be a very safe journey.

The same is true when it comes to investing: just because an investment may have an average return of 8 percent, that doesn't mean it always realizes that rate of return. It's important to remember that an investment's average rate of return doesn't tell you much about its overall volatility.

As you organize your portfolio, it's important to remember the concept of sequence of returns and to avoid the "Flaw of Averages" so you can best balance your Red Money and Green Money.

## HOW REAL PEOPLE MAKE INVESTMENT DECISIONS

It can be challenging to watch the stock market's erratic changes every month, week or even every day. When you have your money riding on it, the ride can feel pretty bumpy. When you are managing your money by yourself, emotions inevitably enter into the mix. The Dow Jones Industrial Average and the S&P 500 represent more to you than market fluctuations. They represent a portion of your retirement. It's hard not to be emotional about it.

Everyone knows you should buy low and sell high. But this is what is more likely to happen:

The market takes a downturn, similar to the 2008 crash, and investors see as much as a 30 percent loss in their stock holdings. It's hard to watch, and it's harder to bear the pain of losing that much money. The math of rebounds means that they will need to rely on even larger gains just to get back to where things were before the downturn. They sell. But eventually, and inevitably, the market begins to rise again. Maybe slowly, maybe with some moderate growth, but by the time the average investor notices an upward trend and wants to buy in again, they have already missed a great deal of the gains.

## THE IMPACT OF VOLATILITY ON THE AVERAGE INVESTOR

» *Betty's situation illustrates how market volatility can have major repercussions for an individual investor. Betty works for Acme Paper Company for 34 years. During her time there, she acquires bonuses and pay raises that often include shares of stock in the company. She also dedicates part of her paycheck every month to a 401(k) that bought Acme stock. By the time she retires, Fran has $250,000 worth of Acme stock.*

*Although she had contributes to her 401(k) account every month, Betty doesn't cultivate any other assets that could generate income for her during retirement. Betty also retires early at age 62 because of her failing health. The commute to work every day was becoming difficult in her weakened condition and she wanted to enjoy the rest of her life in retirement instead of working at Acme.*

*Because she retires early, Betty fails to maximize her Social Security benefit. While she lives a modest lifestyle, her income needs will still be $3,500 per month. Betty's monthly Social Security check will only cover $1,900, leaving her with a $1,600 income gap. To supplement her Social Security check,*

| Portfolio A | | | Portfolio B | |
|---|---|---|---|---|
| Year | Hypothetical stock market gains or losses | | Year | Hypothetical stock market gains or losses |
| 1 | -10.14% | | 1 | 12.78% |
| 2 | -13.04% | | 2 | 23.45% |
| 3 | -23.37% | | 3 | 26.38% |
| 4 | 14.62% | | 4 | 3.53% |
| 5 | 2.03% | | 5 | 13.62% |
| 6 | 12.40% | | 6 | 3.00% |
| 7 | 27.25% | | 7 | -38.49% |
| 8 | -6.56% | | 8 | 26.38% |
| 9 | 26.31% | | 9 | 19.53% |
| 10 | 4.46% | | 10 | 26.67% |
| 11 | 7.06% | | 11 | 31.01% |
| 12 | -1.54% | | 12 | 20.26% |
| 13 | 34.11% | | 13 | 34.11% |
| 14 | 20.26% | | 14 | -1.54% |
| 15 | 31.01% | | 15 | 7.06% |
| 16 | 26.67% | | 16 | 4.46% |
| 17 | 19.53% | | 17 | 26.31% |
| 18 | 26.38% | | 18 | -6.56% |
| 19 | -38.49% | | 19 | 27.25% |
| 20 | 3.00% | | 20 | 12.40% |
| 21 | 13.62% | | 21 | 2.03% |
| 22 | 3.53% | | 22 | 14.62% |
| 23 | 26.38% | | 23 | -23.37% |
| 24 | 23.45% | | 24 | -13.04% |
| 25 | 12.78% | | 25 | -10.14% |
| Avg. Annual Return | 9.69% | | Avg. Annual Return | 9.69% |

*Betty sells $1,600 of her Acme stock each month to meet her income needs. A $250,000 401(k) is nothing to sneeze at, but reducing its value by $1,600 every month will barely last Betty 10 years. And that's if the market stays neutral or grows* *modestly. If the market takes a downturn, the money that Betty relied on to fill her income gap will rapidly diminish. Even if the market starts going up in a couple of years, it will take much larger gains for her to recover the value that she lost.*

*Unhappily for Betty, she retired in 2007, just before the major market downturn that lasted for several years. She lost more than 20 percent of the value of her stock. Because Betty needed to sell her stock to meet her basic income needs, the market price of the stock was secondary to her need for the money. When she needed money, she was forced to sell however many shares she needed to fill her income gap that month. And if she has a financial crisis, involving her need for medical care, for example, she will be forced to sell stock even if the market is low and her shares are nearly worthless.*

*Betty realizes that she could have relied on an investment structured to deliver her a regular income while protecting the value of her investment. She could have kept her $250,000 from diminishing while enjoying her lifestyle into retirement regardless of the volatility of the market. Ideally, Betty would have restructured her 401(k) to reflect the level of risk that she was able to take. In her case, she would have had most of her money in Green Money assets, allowing her to rely on the value of her assets when she needed them.*

## HOW VOLATILITY AFFECTS INVESTOR BEHAVIOR

In 2017, DALBAR, the well-respected financial services market research firm, released their annual "Quantitative Analysis of Investment Behavior" report (QAIB). The report studied the impact of market volatility on individual investors: a person like Betty, or anyone who was managing (or mismanaging) their own investments in the stock market.

According to the study, volatility not only caused investors to make decisions based on their emotions, those decisions also harmed their investments and prevented them from realizing potential gains. So why do people meddle so much with their investments when the market is fluctuating? Part of the reason is that many people have financial obligations that they don't have control over. Significant expenses like house payments, the unexpected cost of replacing a broken-down car, and medical bills can put people in a position where they need money. If they need to sell investments to come up with that money, they don't have the luxury of selling when they *want* to. They must sell when they *need* to.

DALBAR's "Quantitative Analysis of Investor Behavior" has been used to measure the effects of investors' buying, selling and mutual fund switching decisions since 1994. The QAIB shows time and time again over nearly a 20-year period that the average investor earns less, and in many cases, significantly less than the performance of mutual funds suggests. QAIB's goal is to improve independent investor performance and to help financial professionals provide helpful advice and investment strategies that address the concerns and behaviors of the average investor.

An excerpt from the report claims that:

*"QAIB offers guidance on how and where investor behaviors can be improved. No matter what the state of the mutual fund industry, boom or bust: Investment results are more dependent on investor behavior than on fund performance. Mutual fund investors who hold on to their investments are more successful than those who time the market.*

*QAIB uses data from the Investment Company Institute (ICI), Standard & Poor's and Barclays Capital Index Products to compare mutual fund investor returns to an appropriate set of benchmarks.*

*There are actually three primary causes for the chronic shortfall for both equity and fixed income investors:*
1. *Capital not available to invest. This accounts for 25 percent to 35 percent of the shortfall.*
2. *Capital needed for other purposes. This accounts for 35 percent to 45 percent of the shortfall.*
3. *Psychological factors. These account for 45 percent to 55 percent of the shortfall."*

The key findings of DALBAR's QAIB report provide compelling statistics about how individual investment strategies produced negative outcomes for the majority of investors:

- In five out of 12 months, investors guessed right about the market direction the following month. While "guessing right" 42 percent of the time in 2016, the average mutual fund investor was not able to keep pace with the market, based on the actual volume and timing of fund flows

- When looking at the long-term annualized returns of the average equity mutual fund investor compared to the S&P 500 we see that the average investor has always lagged the overall market. While the gap between the average equity mutual fund investor and the S&P 500 has narrowed considerably in the past 15 years, the average investor has earned almost half of what they would have earned by buying and holding an S&P index fund (4.67 percent vs. 8.19 percent).

- No evidence has been found to link predictably poor investment recommendations to average investor underperformance. Analysis of the underperformance shows that investor behavior is the number one cause, with fees being the second leading cause.

- In 2016, the average equity mutual fund investor under-performed the S&P 500 by a margin of 4.70 percent.* It doesn't take a financial services market research report to tell you that market volatility is out of your control. The report does prove, however, that before you experience market volatility, you should have an investment plan, and when the market is fluctuating, you should stand by your investment plan. You should also review and discuss your investment plan with your financial professional on a regular basis, ensuring he/she is aware of any changes in your goals, financial circumstances, your health or your risk tolerance. When the economy is under stress and the markets are volatile, investors can feel vulnerable. That vulnerability causes people to tinker with their portfolios in an attempt to outsmart the market. Financial profes-sionals, however, don't try to time the market for their clients. They try to tap into the gains that can be realized by committing to long-term investment strategies.

---

*2017 QAIB, Dalbar, March 2017*

## CHAPTER 9 RECAP //

- Market downturns hurt everyone's portfolios, but they can have a much bigger impact on retirees. If the timing of a market downturn hits right before or just after you retire, and you haven't sufficiently protected yourself from risk, you could stand to jeopardize the viability of your income plan.
- Additionally, if you are making withdrawals from market investments during a downturn, you can contribute exponentially to the depletion of your assets.
- Emotions and investing go hand in hand for most investors. Money represents a lot of work, time, and hope. When the market suffers a loss, it is hard to keep a level head. The 2017 DALBAR "Quantitative Analysis of Investment Behavior" report highlights that the average fixed-income investor who managed their money by themselves didn't even keep up with inflation in nine out of the last 14 years!

# 10

# THE POWER OF MANAGED MONEY

Now that you've calculated the Rule of 100 (Chapter 2), determined how much risk you have and how much you want, and you've determined how much Green Money you need to meet your short-term and mid-term income needs, it's time to look at what you have left. The money you have left after you've calculated your Green Money needs has the potential of becoming Red Money: your stocks, mutual funds and other investment products that you want to continue accumulating value with the market. You now have the luxury of taking a closer second look at your Red Money to determine how you would like to manage it.

As you read earlier in the key findings of the DALBAR report, the deck is stacked against the individual investor. Remember that the average fixed income investor failed to keep pace with inflation in nine of the last 14 years, meaning the inherent risk in managing your Red Money is very real and could have a lasting impact on your assets. So, how much of your Red Money do you invest, and in what kinds of markets, investment products and stocks do you invest? There are a lot of different directions in which you can take your Red Money. One thing is for sure: significant accumulation depends on investing in the market. How you go about doing it is different for everyone. Gathering stocks, bonds and investment funds together in a portfolio without a cohesive strategy behind them could cause you to miss out on the benefits of a more thoughtful and planful approach. The end result is that you may never really understand what your money is doing, where and how it is really invested, and which investment principles are behind the investment products you hold. While you may have goals for each individual piece of your portfolio, it is likely that you don't have a comprehensive plan for your Red Money, which may mean that *you are taking on more risk than you would like, and are getting less return for it than is possible.*

Enter **Managed Money.** Managed Money is money that is managed by a professional *with a purpose.* After your income needs are met and you have assets that you would like to dedicate to accumulation, there are decisions you need to make about how to invest those assets. You can buy stocks, index funds, mutual funds, bonds—you name it—you can invest in it. However, the difference between Red Money and Managed Money is that Managed Money has a cohesive strategy behind it that is *implemented by a professional.* When you manage your Red Money with an investment plan, it becomes Managed Money: *money that is being managed with a specific purpose, a specific set of focused goals and a specific strategy in mind.* Managed Money is still a type of Red Money. It comes with different levels of risk. But Managed Money is under the watchful eye of professionals who have a stake in the success of your money in the market and who can recommend a range of strategies from those designed for preservation to those targeting rapid growth. You don't want to miss out on achieving the right level of risk, and more importantly, composing a careful plan for the return of your assets.

It can be helpful to think of Red Money and Managed Money with this analogy:

If you needed to travel through an unfamiliar city in a foreign country, you could rent a car or perhaps hire a driver. Were you to drive yourself, you would try to gain guidance from perplexing road signs and need to adhere to traffic rules—with no experience or assistance to lean on. It would take longer to get to where you want to go, and the chance of a traffic accident would be higher. If you hired a driver, they would manage your journey. A driver would know the route, how to avoid traffic, and follow the rules of the road.

Red Money is like driving yourself. With Managed Money, you are still traveling by car, but now you have a professional working on your behalf.

## TAKING A CLOSER LOOK AT YOUR PORTFOLIO

Think about your investment portfolio. Think specifically of what you would consider your Red Money. Do you know what is there? You may have several different investment products like individual mutual funds, bond accounts, stocks, etc. You may have inherited a stock portfolio from a relative, or you might be invested in a bond account offered by the company for which you worked due to your familiarity with them. While you may or may not be managing your investments individually, the reality is that you probably don't have an overall management strategy for all of your investments. Investments that aren't managed are simply Red Money, or money that is at risk in the market.

Harnessing the earning potential of your Red Money relies on more than a collection of stocks and bonds, however. It needs guided management. A good Managed Money manager uses the knowledge they have about the level of risk with which you are comfortable, what you need or want to use your money for, when you want or need it and how you want to use it. The Managed Money objects that they choose for you will still have a certain level of risk, but under the right management, control and process, you have a far better chance of a successful outcome that meets your specific needs.

When you sit down with an investment professional, you can look at all of your assets together. Chances are that you have accumulated a number of different assets over the last 20, 30 or 50 years. You may have a 401(k), an IRA, a Roth IRA, an account of self-directed stocks, a brokerage account, etc. Wherever you put your money, a financial professional will go through your assets and help you determine the level of risk to which you are exposed now and should be exposed in the future.

Here is a typical example of how an investment professional can be helpful to a future retiree with Managed Money needs:

> » *Elizabeth is 65 years old and wants to retire in two years. She has a 401(k) from her job to which she has contributed for 26 years. She also has some stocks that her late husband managed. Elizabeth also has $55,000 in a mutual fund that her sister recommended to her five years ago and $30,000 in another mutual fund that she heard about at work. She takes a look at her assets one day and decides that she doesn't understand what they add up to or what kind of retirement they will provide. She decides to meet with an investment professional. Elizabeth's professional immediately asks her:*
>
> **1. Does she know exactly where all of her money is?**
> *Elizabeth doesn't know much about all her husband's stocks,*

which have now become hers. Their value is at $100,000 invested in three large cap companies. Elizabeth is unsure of the companies and whether she should hold or sell them.

**2. Does she know what types of assets she owns?** Yes and no. She knows she had a 401(k) and IRAs, but she is unfamiliar with her husband's self-directed stock portfolio or the type of mutual funds she owns. Furthermore she is unclear as to how to manage the holdings as she nears retirement.

**3. Does she know the strategies behind each one of the investment products she owns?** While Elizabeth knows she had a 401(k), an IRA and mutual fund holdings, she doesn't know how her 401(k) is organized or how to make it more conservative as she nears retirement. She is unsure whether her IRA is a Roth or traditional variety and how to draw income from them? She really does not have specific investment principles guiding her investment decisions, and she doesn't know anything about her husband's individual stocks. One major concern for Elizabeth is whether her family would be okay if she were not around?

After determining Elizabeth's assets, her financial professional prepares a consolidated report that lays out all of her assets for her to review. Her professional explains each one of them to her. She discovers that although she is two years away from retiring, her 401(k) is organized with an amount of risk with which she is not comfortable. Sixty percent of her 401(k) is at risk, far off the mark if we abide by the Rule of 100. Elizabeth opts to be more conservative than the Rule of 100 suggests, as she will rely on her 401(k) for most of her immediate income needs after retirement. Elizabeth's professional also points out several instances of overlap between her mutual funds. Elizabeth learns that while she is comfortable with one of her mutual funds, she does not agree with the management principles of the other.

*In the end, Elizabeth's professional helps her re-organize her 401(k) to secure her more Green Money for retirement income. They also create a Yellow Money account to meet her liquidity needs. Her professional also uses her mutual fund and her husband's stock assets to create a growth oriented investment plan that Elizabeth will rely on for Need Later Money in 15 years when she plans on relocating closer to her children and grandchildren. By creating an overall investment strategy, Elizabeth is able to meet her targeted goals in retirement. Elizabeth's financial professional worked closely with her and her tax professional to minimize the tax impact of any asset sales on Elizabeth's situation.*

Like Elizabeth, you may have several savings vehicles: a 401(k), an IRA to which you regularly contribute, some mutual funds to which you make monthly contributions, etc. But what is your *overall investment strategy*? Do you have one in place? Do you want one that will help you meet your retirement goals? Managed Money looks at *ALL* your accounts and all their different strategies to create a plan that helps them all work together. Your current investment situation may not reflect your wishes. As a matter of fact, it likely doesn't.

You may have a better understanding of your assets than Elizabeth did, but even someone with an investment strategy can benefit from having a financial professional review their portfolio:

» *Trent is 69 years old. He retired four years ago. He relied on income from an IRA for three years in order to increase his Social Security benefit. He also made significant investments in 36 different mutual funds. He chose to diversify among the funds by selecting a portion for growth, another for good dividends, another that focused on promising small cap companies and a final portion that work like index funds. All the money that Trent had in mutual funds he considered Need Later Money that he wanted to rely on in his 80s. After the stock market took a hit in 2008, Trent lost some confidence in his investments and decided to sit down with a financial professional to see if his portfolio was able to recover.*

*The professional Trent met with was able to determine what goals he had in mind. Specifically, the financial professional determined what Trent actually wanted and needed the money for, and when he needed it. His professional also looked inside each of the mutual funds and discovered several instances of overlap. While Trent had created diversity in his portfolio by selecting funds focused on different goals, he didn't account for overlap in the companies in which the funds were invested. Out of the 36 funds, his professional found that 20 owned nearly identical stock. While most of the companies were good investments, the high instance of overlap did not contribute to the healthy investment diversity that Trent wanted. Trent's financial professional also provided him with a report that explained the concentration ratio of his holdings (noting how much of his portfolio was contained within the top 25 stock holdings), the percentage of his portfolio that each company in which he invested in represented (showing the percentage of net assets that each company made up as an overall position in his portfolio) and the portfolio date of his account (showing when the funds in his portfolio were last updated: as funds are required to report updates only twice per year, it was possible that some of his fund reports could be six months old).*

*Trent's professional consolidated his assets into one investment management strategy. This allowed Trent's investments to be managed by someone he trusted who knew his specific investment goals and needs. Eliminating redundancy and overlap in his portfolio was easy to do but difficult to detect since Trent had multiple funds with multiple brokerage firms. Trent sat down with a professional to see if his mutual funds could perform well, and he left with a consolidated management plan and a money manager that understood him personally. That's Managed Money at its best.*

## AVOIDING EMOTIONAL INVESTING

There's no way around it; people get emotional about their money. And for good reason. You've spent your life working for it, exchanging your time and talent for it, and making decisions about how to invest it, save it and make it grow. The maintenance of your lifestyle and your plans for retirement all depend on it. The best investment strategies, however, don't rely on emotions. One of Managed Money's greatest strengths lies in the fact that it is managed by someone who understands your needs and desires, but doesn't make decisions about your money under the influence of emotion.

A well-managed investment account meets your goals as a whole, not in individualized and piecemeal ways. Professional money managers do this by creating requirements for each type of investment in which they put your money. We'll call them "screens." Your money manager will run your holdings through the screens they have created to evaluate different types of investment strategies. A professionally managed account will only have holdings that meet the requirements laid out in the overall management plan that was designed to meet your investment goals. The holdings that don't make it through the screens, the ones that don't contribute to your investment goals, are sold and redistributed to investments that your financial professional has determined to be appropriate.

Different screens apply to different Managed Money strategies. For example, if one of your goals is significant growth, which would require taking on more risk alongside the potential for more return, an investment professional would screen for companies that have high rates of revenue and sales growth, high earnings growth, rising profit margins, and innovative products. On the other hand, if you want your portfolio to be used for income, which would call for lower risk and less return, your professional would screen for dividend yield and sector diversification. *Every investor has a different goal, and every goal requires a customized strategy that uses quantitative screens.* A professional will create a portfolio that reflects your investment desires. If some of the current assets you own complement the strategies that your professional recommends, those will likely stay in your portfolio.

Screening your assets removes emotions from the equation. It removes attachment to underperforming or overly risky investments. Financial professionals aren't married to particular stocks or mutual funds for any reason. They go by the numbers and see your portfolio through a lens shaped by your retirement goals. Your professional understands your wants and needs, and creates an investment strategy that takes your life events and future plans into account. It's a planful approach, and it allows you to tap into the tools and resources of a professional who has built a career around successful investing. Managing money is a full-time job and is best left to a professional money manager.

Removing emotions from investing also allows you to be unaffected by the day-to-day volatility of the market. Your financial professional doesn't ask where the market is going to be in a year, three years or a month from now. If you look at the value of the stock market from the beginning of the twentieth century to today, it's going up. Despite the Great Depression, despite the 1987 crash, despite the 2008 market downturn, the market, as a whole, trends up. Remember the major market downturn in 2008 when the market lost 30 percent of its value? Not only did it completely recover, it has far exceeded its 2008 value. Emotional investing led countless people to sell low as the market went down, and buy the same shares back when the market started to recover. That's an expensive way to do business. While you can't afford to lose money that you need in two, three or five years, your Need Later Money has time to grow. The best way to do so is to use Managed Money.

## CREATING AN INVESTMENT STRATEGY

It is very likely that you can benefit from taking a more managed investment approach tailored to your goals. Managed Money is generally Need Later Money that you want to grow for needs you'll have in at least 10 years. You can work with your financial planner to create investments that meet your needs within different timeframes. You may need to rely on some of your Managed Money in 10, 15 or 20 years, whether for additional income, a large purchase you plan on making or a vacation. Whatever you want it for, you will need it down the road. A financial professional can help you rescale the risk of your assets as they grow, helping you lock in your profits and secure a source of income you can depend on later.

So what does a Managed Money account look like? Here's what it *doesn't* look like: a portfolio with 49 small cap mutual funds, a dozen individual stocks and an assortment of bond accounts. A brokerage account with a hodgepodge of investments, even if goal-oriented, is not a professionally managed account. It's still Red Money. Remember, Managed Money is a managed account that has an overarching investment philosophy. When you look at making investments that will perform to meet your future income needs, the burning question becomes: How much should you have in the market and how should it be invested? Working with a professional will help you determine how much risk you should take, how to balance your assets so they will meet your goals and how to plan for the big ticket items, like health care expenses, that may be in your future. Yes, Managed Money is exposed to risk, but by working with a professional, you can manage that risk in a productive way.

## WHY MANAGED MONEY?

If you have met your immediate income needs for retirement, why bother with professionally managing your other assets? The money you have accumulated above and beyond your income needs probably has a greater purpose. It may be for your children or grandchildren. You may want to give money to a charity or organization that you admire. In short, you may want to craft your legacy. It would be advantageous to grow your assets in the best manner possible. A financial professional has built a career around managing money in profitable ways. They are experts under the supervision of the organization that they represent.

Turning to Managed Money also means that you don't have to burden yourself with the time commitment, the stress, and the cost of determining how to manage your money. Managed Money can help you better enjoy your retirement. Do you want to sit down in your home office every day and determine how to best allocate your assets, or do you want to be living your life while someone else manages your money for you? When the majority of your Red Money is managed with a specific purpose by a financial professional, you don't have to be worrying about which stocks to buy and sell today or tomorrow.

## SEEKING FINANCIAL ADVICE: STOCK BROKERS VS. INVESTMENT ADVISOR REPRESENTATIVES

Investors basically have access to two types of advice in today's financial world: advice from stock brokers and advice given by investment advisors. Most investors, however, don't know the difference between types of advice and the people from whom they receive advice. Today, there are two primary types of advice offered to investors: advice given by a commission-based registered

145

representative (brokers) and advice given by fee-based Investment Advisor Representatives. Unfortunately, many investors are not aware that a difference exists; nor have they been explained the distinction between the two types of advice. In a survey taken by TD Ameritrade, the top reasons investors choose to work with an independent registered investment advisor are:*

- Registered Investment Advisors are required, as fiduciaries, to offer advice that is in the best interest of clients
- More personalized service and competitive fee structure offered at a Registered Investment Advisor firm
- Dissatisfaction with full commission brokers

The truth is that there is a great deal of difference between stock brokers and investment advisor representatives. For starters, investment advisor representatives are obligated to act in an investor's best interests in any and all aspects of a financial relationship. Confusion continues to exist among investors struggling to find the best financial advice out there and the most credible sources of advice.

Here is some information to help clear up the confusion so you can find good advice from a professional you can trust:

- Investment advisor representatives have the fiduciary duty to act in a client's best interest at all times with every investment decision they make. Stock brokers and brokerage firms usually do not act as fiduciaries to their investors and are not obligated to make decisions that are entirely in the best interest of their customers. For example, if you decide you want to invest in precious metals, a stock broker would offer you a precious metals account from their firm. An Investment Advisor would find you a precious

---

* *2011 Advisor Sentiment Study, commissioned by TD AMERITRADE. TD Ameritrade, Inc.*

metals account that is the best fit for you based on the investment strategy of your portfolio.

- Investment advisors give their clients a Form ADV describing the methods that the professional uses to do business. An Investment Advisor also obtains client consent regarding any conflicts of interest that could exist with the business of the professional.
- Stock brokers and brokerage firms are not obligated to provide comparable types of disclosure to their customers.
- Whereas stock brokers and firms routinely earn large profits by trading as principal with customers, Investment Advisors cannot trade with clients as principal (except in very limited and specific circumstances).
- Investment Advisors charge a pre-negotiated fee with their clients in advance of any transactions. They cannot earn additional profits or commissions from their customers' investments without prior consent. Registered Investment Advisors are commonly paid an asset-based fee that aligns their interests with those of their clients. Brokerage firms and stock brokers, on the other hand, have much different payment agreements. Their revenues may increase regardless of the performance of their customers' assets.
- Unlike brokerage firms, where investment banking and underwriting are commonplace, Registered Investment Advisors must manage money in the best interests of their customers. Because Registered Investment Advisors charge set fees for their services, their focus is on their client. Brokerage firms may focus on other aspects of the firm that do not contribute to the improvement of their clients' assets.
- Unlike brokers, Registered Investment Advisors do not get commissions from fund or insurance companies for selling their investment products.

Just to drive home the point, here is what a fiduciary duty to a client means for a Registered Investment Advisor. Registered Investment Advisors must:*

- Always act in the best interest of their client and make investment decisions that reflect their goals.
- Identify and monitor securities that are illiquid.
- When appropriate, employ fair market valuation procedures.
- Observe procedures regarding the allocation of investment opportunities, including new issues and the aggregation of orders.
- Have policies regarding affiliated broker-dealers and maintenance of brokerage accounts.
- Disclose all conflicts of interest.
- Have policies on use of brokerage commissions for research.
- Have policies regarding directed brokerage, including step-out trades and payment for order flow.
- Abide by a code of ethics.

---

* *2011 Advisor Sentiment Study, commissioned by TD AMERITRADE. TD Ameritrade, Inc.*

## CHAPTER 10 RECAP //

- Managed Money is overseen by a financial professional. It is technically considered a Red Money asset, but it is managed with a purpose and a strategy that has a specific goal. This type of management can reduce some of the risk of investing in the market.
- Red Money is like taking a road trip without a map. Managed Money, however, is like handing the wheel over to someone who has driven the route before and knows all the shortcuts and the good places to eat along the way.
- Emotions can have a negative impact on the average investor's financial decisions. Decisions about managed money are made without emotions. A financial professional relies on data and criteria designed for your retirement plan to make decisions about the investment.

# 11
# NEW IDEAS FOR INVESTING

*How important is Yellow Money?*

In Chapter 2, we discussed how today investment options requires advice that is relevant to today. Traditional, outdated investment strategies are not only ineffective, they can be harmful to the average investor. One of the most traditional ways of thinking about investing is the risk versus reward trade-off. It goes something like this.

Investment options that are considered safer carry less risk, but also offer the potential for less return. Riskier investment options carry the burden of volatility and a greater potential for loss, but they also offer a greater potential for large rewards. Most professionals move their clients back and forth along this range, shifting between investments that are safer and investments that are structured for growth. Essentially, the old rules of investing dictate that you can either choose relative safety *or* return, but you can't have both.

Updated investment strategies work with the flexibility of liquidity to remake the rules. Here is how:

There are three dimensions that are inherent in any investment: *Liquidity, Safety,* and *Return.* You can maximize any two of these dimensions at the expense of the third. If you choose Safety and Liquidity, this is like keeping your assets in a checking account or savings account. This option delivers a lot of Safety and Liquidity, but at the expense of any Return. On the other hand, if you choose Liquidity and Return, meaning you have the potential for great return and can still reclaim your money whenever you choose, you will likely be exposed to a very high level of risk.

Understanding Liquidity can help you break the old Risk versus Safety trade-off. By identifying assets from which you don't require Liquidity, you can place yourself in a position to potentially profit from relatively safe investments that provide a higher than average rate of return.

Choosing Safety and Return over Liquidity can have significant impacts on the accumulation of your assets. In Ted's case, the paradigm shift from earning and saving to leveraging assets was a costly one.

> » *Ted is a corn and soybean farmer with 1,200 acres of land. He routinely retains somewhere between $40,000 and $80,000 in his checking and savings accounts. If a major piece of equipment fails and needs repair or replacement, Ted will need the money available to pay for the equipment and carry on with farming. If the price of feed for his cattle goes up one year, he will need to compensate for the increased overhead to his farming operation. He isn't a particularly wealthy farmer, but he has little choice but to keep a portion of money on hand in case something comes up and he must*

*access it quickly. Most of his capital is held in livestock in the pasture or crops in the ground tied up for six to eight months of the year. When a major financial need arises, Ted can't just harvest 10 acres of soybeans and use them for payment. He needs to depend heavily on Liquidity in order to be a successful farmer.*

*Old habits die hard, however, and when Ted finally hangs up his overalls and quits farming, he keeps his bank accounts flush with cash, just like in the old days. After selling the farm and the equipment, Ted keeps a huge portion of the profits in Liquid investments because that's what he is familiar with. Unfortunately for Ted, with his pile of money sitting in his checking account, he isn't even keeping pace with inflation. After all his hard work as a farmer, his money is losing value every day because he didn't shift to a paradigm of leveraging his assets to generate income and accumulate value.*

*Almost anything would be a better option for Ted than clinging to Liquidity. He could have done something better to get either more return from his money or more safety, and at the very least would not have lost out to inflation.*

As you can see, choosing Liquidity solely can be a costly option. The sooner you want your money back, the less you can leverage it for Safety or Return. If you have the option of putting your money in a long-term investment, you will be sacrificing Liquidity, but potentially gaining both Safety and Return. Rethinking your approach to money in this way can make a world of difference and can provide you with a structured way to generate income while allowing the value of your asset to grow over time.

## TAKING ANOTHER LOOK AT YOUR YELLOW MONEY

You need a plan that works for you the day you retire, and you need a plan that works for you 15, 20, and 30 years down the road. Your plan needs to be a living thing that adapts to your life. While retirement may seem like a static period where your expenses, interests, and priorities remain the same, that is almost never the case. Marriages, babies, divorces, travel, homes, and a long list of other things can come and go over the span of a retirement. Your car might need new tires or an expensive repair, or you might want to build a new fence in your backyard. Updating your plan along the way can help you account for these changes, and anticipate ones in the future.

Updating your plan means you'll need to work with a financial professional who is willing and able to meet with you to make changes. They will need to be paying attention to your portfolio, your life, and your overall plan each month and year. When you have questions about what to do, it is imperative that the person you consult is up to date on your life and your finances.

Preparing for unexpected future expenses often requires some of your assets to be liquid, or Yellow Money assets. Having the convenience and flexibility of liquidity can help protect you from unnecessary fees, tax liabilities, and other drawbacks from accessing other non-liquid accounts.

**The question is, how much Liquidity do you *really* need?** Think about it. If you haven't sat down and created an income plan for your retirement, your perceived need for Liquidity is a guess. You don't know how much cash you'll need to fill the income gap if you don't know the amount of your Social Security benefit of the total of your other income options. If you *have* determined your income need and have made a plan for filling your income gap, you can partition your assets based on when you will need them. With an income plan in place, *you can use new rules to enjoy both Safety and Return from your assets.*

## CHAPTER 11 RECAP //

- Investments have three main qualities: liquidity, safety, and return. Choosing to maximize two qualities diminishes the third.
- Liquidity is important, but too much liquidity can cost you. More liquidity means less leverage for safety and return on your investment. A flexible retirement plan requires a creative approach to these three qualities.
- A good retirement plan isn't a "one and done" thing. You need to create a plan that adapts with your life. Your plan should be reviewed and updated by both you and your financial professional on a regular basis to make sure your current and anticipated needs are met.

# 12

# TAXATION WITHOUT COMPLICATION

*Create an efficient tax plan before you retire.*

Taxes play a starring role in the theater of retirement planning. Everyone is familiar with taxes (you've been paying them your entire working life), but not everyone is familiar with how to make tax planning a part of their retirement strategy.
Taxes are taxes, right? You'll pay them before retirement and you'll pay them during retirement. What's the difference? The truth is that a planful approach to taxes can help you save money, protect your assets and ensure that your legacy remains intact.

How can a tax form do all that? The answer lies in planning. *Tax planning* and *tax reporting* are two very different things.

Most people only *report* their taxes. March rolls around, people pull out their 1040s or use TurboTax to enter their income and taxable assets, and ship it off to Uncle Sam at the IRS. If you use a CPA to report your taxes, you are essentially paying them to record history. You have the option of being proactive with your taxes and to plan for your future by making smart, informed decisions about how taxes affect your overall financial plan. Working with a financial professional who, along with a CPA, makes recommendations about your finances to you, will keep you looking forward instead of in the rearview mirror as you enter retirement.

## TAXES AND RETIREMENT

When you retire, you move from the earning and accumulation phase of your life into the asset distribution phase of your life. For most people, that means relying on Social Security, a 401(k), an IRA, or a pension. Wherever you have put your Green Money for retirement, you are going to start relying on it to provide you with the income that once came as a paycheck. Most of these distributions will be considered income by the IRS and will be taxed as such. There are exceptions to that (not all of your Social Security income is taxed, and income from Roth IRAs is not taxed), but for the most part, your distributions will be subject to income taxes.

Regarding assets that you have in an IRA or a 401(k) plan that uses an IRA, when you reach 70 ½ years of age, you will be required to draw a certain amount of money from your IRA as income each year. That amount depends on your age and the balance in your IRA. The amount that you are required to withdraw as income is called a Required Minimum Distribution (RMD). Why are you required to withdraw money from your own account? Chances are the money in that account has grown over time, and the government wants to collect taxes on that growth. If you have a large balance in an IRA, there's a chance your RMD could increase your income significantly enough to put you into a higher tax bracket, subjecting you to a higher tax rate.

Here's where tax planning can really begin to work strongly in your favor. In the distribution phase of your life, you have a predictable income based on your RMDs, your Social Security benefit and any other income-generating assets you may have. What really impacts you at this stage is how much of that money you keep in your pocket after taxes. Essentially, *you will make more money saving on taxes than you will by making more money.* If you can reduce your tax burden by 30, 20 or even 10 percent, you earn yourself that much more money by not paying it in taxes.

How do you save money on taxes? By having a plan. In this instance, a financial professional can work with the CPAs at their firm to create a **distribution plan** that minimizes your taxes and maximizes your annual net income.

## BUILDING A TAX DIVERSIFIED PORTFOLIO

So far so good: avoid taxes, maximize your net annual income and have a plan for doing it. When people decide to leverage the experience and resources of a financial professional, they may not be thinking of how distribution planning and tax planning will benefit their portfolios. Often more exciting prospects like planning income annuities, investing in the market and structuring investments for growth rule the day. Taxes, however, play a crucial role in retirement planning. Achieving those tax goals requires knowledge of options, foresight and professional guidance.

Finding the path to a good tax plan isn't always a simple task. Every tax return you file is different from the one before it because things constantly change. Your expenses change. Planned or unplanned purchases occur. Health care costs, medical bills, an inheritance, property purchases, reaching an age where your RMD kicks in or travel, any number of things can affect how much income you report and how many deductions you take each year.

Preparing for the ever-changing landscape of your financial life requires a tax-diversified portfolio that can be leveraged to balance the incomes, expenditures and deductions that affect you each year. A financial professional will work with you to answer questions like these:

- What does your tax landscape look like?
- Do you have a tax-diversified portfolio robust enough to adapt to your needs?
- Do you have a diversity of taxable and non-taxable income planned for your retirement?
- Will you be able to maximize your distributions to take advantage of your deductions when you retire?
- Is your portfolio strong enough and tax-diversified enough to adapt to an ever-changing (and usually increasing) tax code?

» *When Maxine returns home after a week in the hospital recovering from a knee replacement, the 77-year-old calls her daughter, sister and brother to let them know she is home and feeling well. She also should have called her CPA. Maxine's medical expenses for the procedure, her hospital stay, her medications and the ongoing physical therapy she attended amount to more than $50,000.*

*Americans can deduct medical expenses that are more than 10 percent of their Adjusted Gross Income (AGI). Maxine's AGI is $60,000 the year of her knee replacement, meaning she is able to deduct $45,500 of her medical bills from her taxes that year.* \* *Her AGI dictated that she could deduct more*

---

\* *This scenario presumes permanent laws in effect subsequent to 12/31/16*

*than 80 percent of her medical expenses that year. **Maxine
didn't know this**.*

*Had she been working with a financial professional
who regularly asked her about any changes in her life, her
spending, or her expenses (expected or unexpected), Maxine
could have saved thousands of dollars. Maxine can also file
an amendment to her tax return to recoup the overpayment.*

This relatively simple example of how tax planning can save you
money is just the tip of the iceberg. No one can be expected to
know the entire U.S. tax code. But a professional who is working
with a team of CPAs and financial professionals have an advantage over the average taxpayer who must start from square one on
their own every year. Have you been taking advantage of all the
deductions that are available to you?

## PROACTIVE TAX PLANNING

The implications of proactive tax planning are far reaching, and are
larger than many people realize. Remember, doing your taxes in
January, February, March or April means you are writing a history
book. Planning your taxes in October, November or December
means that you are writing the story as it happens. You can look at
all the factors that are at play and make decisions that will impact
your tax return *before* you file it.

Realizing that tax planning is an aspect of financial planning is
an important leap to make. When you incorporate tax planning
into your financial planning strategy, it becomes part of the way
you maximize your financial potential. Paying less in taxes means
you keep more of your money. Simply put, the more money you
keep, the more of it you can leverage as an asset. This kind of
planning can affect you at any stage of your life. If you are 40
years old, are you contributing the maximum amount to your
401(k) plan? Are you contributing to a Roth IRA? Are you finding

ways to structure the savings you are dedicating to your children's education? Do you have life insurance? Taxes and tax planning affects all of these investment tools. Having a relationship with a professional who works with a CPA can help you build a truly comprehensive financial plan that not only works with your investments, but also shapes your assets to find the most efficient ways to prepare for tax time. There may be years that you could benefit from higher distributions because of the tax bracket that you are in, or there could be years you would benefit from taking less. There may be years when you have a lot of deductions and years you have relatively few. **Adapting your distributions to work in concert with your available deductions** is at the heart of smart tax planning. Professional guidance can bring you to the next level of income distribution, allowing you to remain flexible enough to maximize your tax efficiency. And remember, saving money on taxes makes you more money than making money does.

What you have on paper is important: your assets, savings, investments, which are financial expression of your work and time. It's just as important to know how to get it off the paper in a way that keeps most of it in your pocket. Almost anything that involves financial planning also involves taxes. Annuities, investments, IRAs, 401(k)s, 403(b), and many other investment options will have tax implications. Life also has a way of throwing curveballs. Illness, expensive car repair or replacement, or *any event that has a financial impact on your life will likely have a corresponding tax implication* around which you should adapt your financial plan. Tax planning does just that.

**One dollar can end up being less than 25 cents to your heirs.**

> » *When Frank's father passed away, he discovered that he was the beneficiary of his father's $500,000 IRA. Frank has a wife and a family of four children, and he knew that his fa-*

*ther had intended for a large portion of the IRA to go toward funding their college educations.*

*After Frank's father's estate is distributed, Frank, who is 50 years old and whose two oldest sons are entering college, liquidates the IRA. By doing so, his taxable income for that year puts him in a 39.6 percent tax bracket, immediately reducing the value of the asset to $302,000. An additional 3.8 percent surtax on net investment income further diminishes the funds to $283,000. Liquidating the IRA in effect subjects much of Frank's regular income to the surtax, as well. At this point, Frank will be taxed at 43.4 percent.*

*Frank's state taxes are an additional 9 percent. Moreover, estate taxes on Frank's father's assets claim another 22 percent. By the time the IRS is through, Frank's income from the IRA will be taxed at 75 percent, leaving him with $125,000 of the original $500,000. While it would help contribute to the education of his children, it wouldn't come anywhere near completely paying for it, something the $500,000 could have easily done.*

As the above example makes clear, leaving an asset to your beneficiaries can be more complicated than it may seem. In the case of a traditional IRA, after federal, estate and state taxes, the asset could literally diminish to as little as 25 percent of its value.

How does working with a professional help you make smarter tax decisions with your own finances? Any financial professional worth their salt will be working with a firm that has a team of trained tax professionals, including CPAs, who have an intimate knowledge of the tax code and how to adapt a financial plan to it.

Here's another example of how taxes have major implications on asset management:

» *Rex and Lauren, a 62-year-old couple, begin working with a financial professional in October. After structuring their assets to reflect their risk tolerance and creating assets that would provide them Green Money income during retirement, they feel good about their situation. They make decisions that allow them to maximize their Social Security benefits, they have plenty of options for filling their income gap, and have begun a safe yet ambitious Managed Money strategy with their professional. When their professional asks them about their tax plan, they tell him their CPA handled their taxes every year, and did a great job. Their professional says, "I don't mean who does your taxes, I mean, who does your tax planning?" Rex and Lauren aren't sure how to respond.*

*Their professional brings Rex and Lauren's financial plan to the firm's CPA and has her run a tax projection for them. A week later their professional calls them with a tax plan for the year that will save them more than $3,000 on their tax return. The couple is shocked. A simple piece of advice from the CPA based on the numbers revealed that if they paid their estimated taxes before the end of the year, they would be able to itemize it as a deduction, allowing them to save thousands of dollars.*

This solution won't work for everyone, and it may not work for Rex and Lauren every year. That's not the point. By being proactive with their approach to taxes and using the resources made available by their financial professional, they were able to create a tax plan that saved them money.

## MANAGED MONEY AND TAXES

There are also tax implications for the money that you have managed professionally. People with portions of their investment portfolio that are actively traded can particularly benefit from having a proactive tax strategy. Without going into too much detail, for tax purposes there are two kinds of investment money: qualified and non-qualified. Different investment strategies can have different effects on how you are taxed on your investments and the growth of your investments. Some are more beneficial for one kind of investment strategy over another. Determining how to plan for the taxation of non-qualified and qualified investments is fodder for holiday party discussions at accounting firms. While it may not be a stimulating topic for the average investor, you don't have to understand exactly how it works in order to benefit from it.

While there are many differences between qualified and non-qualified investments, the main difference is this: qualified plans are designed to give investors tax benefits by deferring taxation of their growth until they are withdrawn. Non-qualified investments are not eligible for these deferral benefits. As such, non-qualified investments are taxed whenever income is realized from them in the form of growth.

Actively and non-actively traded investments provide a simple example of how to position your investments for the best tax advantage. In an actively traded and managed portfolio, there is a high amount of buying and selling of stocks, bonds, funds, ETFs, etc. If that active portfolio of non-qualified investments does well and makes a 20 percent return one year and you are in the 39.6 percent tax bracket, your net gain from that portfolio is only about 12 percent (39.6 percent tax of the 20 percent gain is roughly 8 percent.) In a passive trading strategy, you can use a qualified investment tool, such as an IRA, to achieve 13, 14 or 15 percent growth (much lower than the actively traded portfolio), but still realize a higher net return because the growth of the qualified investment is not taxed until it is withdrawn.

Does this mean that you have to always rely on a buy and hold strategy in qualified investment tools? Not necessarily. The question is, if you have qualified and non-qualified investments, where do you want to position your actively traded and managed assets? Incorporating a planful approach to positioning your investments for more beneficial taxation can be done many ways, but let's consider one example. Keeping your actively managed investment strategies inside an IRA or some other qualified plan could allow you to realize the higher gains of those investments without paying tax on their growth every year. Your more passively managed funds could then be kept in taxable, non-qualified vehicles and methods, and because you aren't realizing income from them on an annual basis by frequently trading them, they grow sheltered from taxation.

If you are interested in taking advantage of tax strategies that maximize your net income, you need the attentive strategies, experience and knowledge of a professional who can give you options that position you for profit. At the end of the day, what's important to you as the consumer is how much you keep, your after-tax take home.

## ESTATE TAXES

The government doesn't just tax your income from investments while you're alive. They will also dip into your legacy.

While estate taxes aren't as hot of a topic as they were a few years ago, they are still an issue of concern for many people with assets. While taxes may not apply on estates that are less than $5 million, certain states have estate taxes with much lower exclusion ratios. Some are as low as $600,000. Many people may have to pay a state estate tax. One strategy for avoiding those types of taxes is to move assets outside of your estate. That can include gifting them to family or friends, or putting them into an irrevocable trust. Life insurance is another option for protecting your legacy.

## CHAPTER 12 RECAP //

- Withdrawing or moving assets from a 401(k) or IRA for income can have tax repercussions that you need to be aware of. Any decision you make about taking income from these accounts should be an informed one that takes taxable events into account. Any qualified money is taxed immediately upon distribution.
- IRAs are subject to Required Minimum Distributions (RMDs) when participants turn age 70 ½. The federal government requires you to take your RMD. If you fail to, penalties and fees can cost you thousands of dollars each year.
- Even though you're finished with your working years, your retirement income from IRAs, 401(k)s, and other sources is still subject to taxation. Understanding the tax implications of your income can help you create a tax-efficient plan that protects your assets.

# 13
# TAXES AND THE FUTURE

## THE FUTURE OF U.S. TAXATION

Although the phrase "nothing is certain except for death and taxes" is most famously attributed to Benjamin Franklin, variations of this saying existed even before the country's first taxes were levied, and these words continue to ring true to this day. However, due to recent upheavals in the American financial landscape, this saying might need to be modified to, "nothing is certain except for death and *increasing* taxes."

Since 2007, the federal debt held by the public has more than doubled relative to the size of the U.S. economy*. With the wellbeing of the economy in jeopardy, legislation regarding debt reduction and tax reform has become a hot button issue.

---

* *https://www.cbo.gov/publication/52142*

Regardless of what legislation has been, or will be, thrown at the American public, the truth of the matter remains the same: the country's current tax revenues cannot cover its obligations.

If the government wants to keep the lights on, it's going to need more income, which not only means that you can count on being taxed, but also on being taxed at an increasing rate.

## DEBT CEILING – CAUSE AND EFFECTS

Since 2000, Congress has raised the debt ceiling more than a dozen times. Increasing the debt ceiling is needed because the government keeps maxing out its credit limit, which it has been reliant upon since the beginning of the Industrial Revolution. Essentially, each time the federal government reaches the end of its line of credit; Congress raises the debt ceiling to extend it. This type of poor money management behavior is nothing new for many Americans: many people overuse their credit cards and rack up an impressive amount of debt. However, most people do not have the ability to raise the credit limit on a card once they have maxed it out—unless they can show they have the ability to pay the balance back. The only way to pay a credit line back is by making more money than you're spending. In other words, responsibility and a balanced budget are critical components to repaying a debt.

The federal government keeps finding ways to increase its credit line without also finding ways to proportionally cut its spending. Although some spending cuts have been put in place, they are not large enough to be worthy adversaries of the current debt situation. Consequently, the continual increasing of the debt ceiling has raised more than just the ability of the federal government to go further into debt; it has also raised concerns and fears about the direction in which the economy is heading. As investors' worry about the impact that future investment valuations may have on their personal wealth grows progressively serious, the market continues to swing unpredictably.

The truth of the matter is that raising the debt ceiling is only one part of the equation required to address the country's debt problem—tax reform is the other. If the government wants to try to staunch the flow of its ever-rising debt, then it will need to make more money, and the only way the government makes money is by collecting taxes. Unfortunately, however, the government frequently collects less than it spends: the Congressional Budget Office (CBO) estimated the 2017 budget deficit would be $559 billion.*

## DEBT AND EARNINGS

Currently, the national debt is increasing at an unprecedented rate, rising to levels never seen before and threatening serious harm to the economy. In October 2004, the national debt was $7.4 trillion**, and by April 2017 it had climbed to nearly $20 trillion***, which means the national debt grew 270.3 percent during this time period. To further understand the gravity of this situation, consider that economists believe that a sustainable economy's debt exists at a maximum level of approximately 80 percent. In 2014, the U.S. national debt was 101.8 percent of the GDP.**** By 2017, the U.S. national debt has risen to 104.3 percent of the GDP.*****

The significance of these two numbers lies within the contrast. The national debt is the amount that needs to be repaid; this can be thought of as the government's credit card balance. The GDP

---

* https://www.cbo.gov/publication/52370

** CBO, An Update to the Budget and Economic Outlook: 2014 - 2024

*** US Department of the Treasury's Bureau of the Fiscal Service, www.treasurydirect.gov/NP/debt/current

**** Federal Reserve Bank of St Louis Economic Research

***** Federal Reserve Bank of St Louis Economic Research, https://fred.stlouisfed.org/series/GFDEGDQ188S

represents the market value of all goods and services produced within a country during a given period. In other words, the GDP represents the gross taxable income available to the government. If debts are increasing at a rate greater than the gross income available for taxation, then the only way to make up the difference is to increase the rate at which the gross income is being taxed.

Even more concerning is that the disparity between growth in national debt and growth in GDP is projected to continue, which means the amount of money the federal government owes will far outpace its ability to repay it. As anyone who has struggled with debt can tell you, continually borrowing more money than you make can have potentially disastrous consequences.

Unfortunately, analysis of the federal government's budget also shows that regardless of revenue collection rates and increased taxes, the deficit will most likely continue to increase, and without additional spending cuts to help bring the budget into balance, tax increases are likely to continue.

## THE END OF AN ERA

From a historical point of view, taxes are extremely low. The last time the U.S. national debt was even close to the same percentage level of GDP as it is today was for several years after the end of World War II. The maximum tax rate at that point, and through the years from 1944 through 1963, averaged 90 percent. Compare that to the maximum rate of 39.6 percent today, and it becomes very clear that there is a disparity of extreme proportion.

Taxes during this historical period were at extreme levels for nearly 20 years, throughout and following this level of debt-to-GDP. A significant point to note about the difference at that time versus where we are today is the economic activity. The period of 1944 through 1963 was in the heart of both the Industrial Revolution and the birth of the baby-boom generation. Today, we are mired in extreme volatility with frequent periods of boom and bust accompanied by the beginning of the greatest retirement wave ever experienced within the U.S. economy.

To contrast these two time periods with respect to the recovery period is almost asinine, as the external pressures from globalization and domestic unfunded liabilities did not exist or were irrelevant factors during the prior period.

To add insult to injury, U.S. domestic unfunded liabilities were estimated to be about $84 trillion in 2012 and that number has only increased through the intervening years*. These liabilities exist outside of the annual budgetary debt discussed above and are due to items such as Social Security, Medicare and government pensions. The most concerning part of this stems from the fact that we are on the cusp of the greatest retirement wave in U.S. history as the baby-boom generation begins retiring and drawing from the unfunded Social Security for which they currently have entitlement. Over the long-run, expenditures related to healthcare programs such as Medicare and Medicaid are projected to grow faster than the economy overall as the population matures.

To put unfunded liabilities into perspective, consider these as off-balance-sheet obligations similar to those of Enron. Although these are not listed as part of the national debt, they must be paid just the same. The difference between Enron and the U.S. unfunded liabilities is that if the U.S. government cannot come up with the funds to pay all these liabilities through revenue generation then they will print the money necessary to pay the debt.

## WHAT DOES THE SOLUTION LOOK LIKE?

Unfortunately, the general public is in a no-win situation for this solution to the problem. Printing money does not bode well for economic growth as this action creates inflationary pressures that

---

*National Center for Policy Analysis, How Much Does the Federal Government Owe?, June 2012

devalue the U.S. dollar and make everyone less wealthy. Cutting the entitlements that compose this liability leaves millions of people without benefits they have come to expect. The only other option, and one that the government knows all too well, is increased taxes. In fact, according to a Congressional Budget Office paper issued in 2004*, unfunded liabilities are addressed as follows:

*"The term 'unfunded liability' has been used to refer to a gap between the government's projected financial commitment under a particular program and the revenues that are expected to be available to fund that commitment. But no government obligation can be truly considered 'unfunded' because of the U.S. government's sovereign power to tax—which is the ultimate resource to meet its obligations."*

A balanced budget is going to be required at some point and with this will come higher taxes. Given our current position and projected budgets, it is likely that tax increases are coming in the near future. However, although raising taxes is a strategy to raise money, it is not a solution to the government's current and pending fiscal problems.

How do you prepare? Why spend so much time reassuring you that taxes will increase? Because you have an opportunity to take action. Now is the time to prepare for what is to come by structuring countermeasures for the good, the bad, and the ugly of each of these legislative nightmares through tax-advantaged retirement planning.

The truth of the matter is that you make more money by saving on taxes than you do by making more money. The simplistic logic of this statement makes sense when you discover it takes a $1.50 in earnings to put that same dollar, saved in taxes, back in

---

* *CBO paper, Measures of the U.S. Government's Fiscal Position Under Current Law,* Sept. 2004

your pocket*. This simple concept becomes extremely valuable to people in retirement and those living on fixed incomes.

As simple as it sounds, it is much more difficult to execute. Most people fail to put together a plan as they near retirement, beginning with a simple cash flow budget. If you have not analyzed your proposed income streams and expenses, you could not possibly have taken the time to position these cash flows and other events into a tax-preferred plan.

Most people will state, "I have a plan" and thus, they do not need any further assistance in this area. The truth in most instances is that many of these people could not show you their plan, and of the few that could, they would not be able to show you how they have executed it. In this regard, they may as well be Richard Nixon saying, "I am not a crook" for as much as they claim, "I have a plan." The truth lies in waiting.

As you approach or begin retirement, you should look at what cash flows you will have. Do you have a pension? How about Social Security? How much additional cash flow are you going to need to draw from your assets to maintain the lifestyle that you desire?

Most people spend their whole lives saving and accumulating wealth but very little time determining a strategy that will distribute this accumulation in ways that will help them to retain it. You need to make sure you have the appropriate diversification of taxable versus non-taxable assets to complement your distribution strategy.

## THE BENEFITS OF DIVERSIFICATION

Heading into retirement, you should be situated within a diversified tax landscape. The point to spending your whole life accumulating wealth is not to see how big the number is on paper, but

---

*Assuming a 33 percent effective tax rate*

rather to be an exercise in how much you put in your pocket after removing it from the paper.

To truly understand tax diversification, you must understand what types of money exist and how each of these will be treated during accumulation and, most importantly, during distribution. The following is a brief summary:

1. Free money
2. Tax-advantaged money
3. Tax-deferred money
4. Taxable money
   a. Ordinary income
   b. Capital gains and qualified dividends

## FREE MONEY

Free money is the best kind of money regardless of the tax treatment, because in the end you have more money than you would have otherwise. Many employers will provide contributions toward employee retirement accounts to offer additional employment benefits and inspire employees to save for their own retirement. With this, employers often will offer a matching contribution in which they will contribute up to a certain percentage of an employee's salary, generally three to five percent, to that employee's retirement account when the employee contributes to their retirement account as well. For example, if an employee earns $50,000 annually and contributes three percent ($1,500) to their retirement account annually, the employer will also contribute three percent ($1,500) to the employee's account. That is $1,500 in free money. Take all that you can get!

## TAX-ADVANTAGED MONEY

Tax-advantaged money is the next best thing to free-money. Although you have to earn tax-advantaged money you do not have to give part of it away to Uncle Sam. Tax-advantaged money comes in three basic forms that you can utilize during your life-time; four if prison inspires your future, but it's not necessary to discuss that option.

One of the most commonly known forms of tax-advantaged money is municipal bonds, which earn and pay interest that could be federally tax-advantaged, state tax-advantaged, or both state and federal tax-advantaged. There are several caveats that should be discussed in regard to the notion of tax-advantaged income from municipal bonds. First, you will notice that tax-advantaged has several flavors from the state and federal perspective. This is because states will generally tax the interest earned on a municipal bond unless the bond is offered from an entity located within that state. This severely limits the availability of completely tax-advantaged municipal bonds and constrains underlying risk and liquidity factors. Second, municipal bond interest gets added back into the equation for determining your modified adjusted gross income (MAGI) for Social Security and could push your income above the thresholds subjecting a portion of your Social Security income to taxation. In effect, if this interest subjects some other income to taxation then this interest is truly being taxed. Last, municipal bond interest may be excluded from the regular federal tax system, but it is included for determining tax under the alternative minimum tax (AMT) system. In its basic form, the AMT system is a separate tax system that applies if the tax computed under AMT exceeds the tax computed under the regular tax system, the difference between these two computations is the alternative minimum tax.

## TAX-FREE MONEY: ROTH IRA

Roth accounts are probably the single greatest tax asset that has come from Congress outside of life insurance and are well known but rarely used. Roth IRAs were first established by the Taxpayer Relief Act of 1997 and were named after Senator William Roth, the chief sponsor of the legislation. A Roth account is simply an account in the form of an IRA or an employer-sponsored retirement account that allows for tax-advantaged growth of earnings and, thus, tax-advantaged income.

The main difference between a Roth and a traditional IRA or employer-sponsored plan lies within the timing of the taxation. You're probably very familiar with the typical scenario of putting money away for retirement through an employer plan, whereby your employer deducts money from each paycheck and puts it directly into a retirement account. This money is taken out before taxes are calculated meaning you do not pay tax on those earnings today. A Roth account, on the other hand, takes the money *after* the taxes have been taken out and then puts it into the retirement account, so you do pay tax on the money today. The other significant difference between these two is taxation during distribution in later years. With a traditional retirement account, when you take the money out later it gets added to your ordinary income and is taxed accordingly. Additionally, including this in your income subjects you to the consequences previously mentioned for municipal bonds with Social Security taxation, AMT, as well as higher Medicare premiums. A Roth, on the other hand, has tax-advantaged distributions and does not contribute toward negative impact items such as Social Security taxation, AMT, or Medicare premium increases. It essentially comes back to you without tax and other obligations.

The best way to consider the difference between the two accounts is to look at the life of a farmer. A farmer will buy seed, plant it in the ground, grow the crops, and harvest it later for sale. Typically, the farmer would only pay tax on the crops that have been harvested and sold. But if you were the farmer, would you rather pay tax on $5,000 worth of seed that you plant today or $50,000 worth of harvested crop later? The obvious answer is $5,000 worth of seed today. The truth of the matter is that you are a farmer, except you are planting dollars into your retirement account instead of seeds into the earth.

So why doesn't everyone have a Roth retirement account if things are so simple? There are several reasons, but the single greatest reason has been the constraints on contributions. If you earned over certain thresholds (MAGI over $133,000 single and $196,000 joint for 2017), you were not eligible to make contributions, and, until 2010, if your modified adjusted gross income (MAGI) was over $100,000 (single or joint) then you could not convert a traditional IRA to a Roth. Outside of these contribution limits, most people save for retirement through their employers and most employers are not offering Roth options within their plans. The reason behind this is because Roth accounts are not that well understood and people have been educated to believe that saving on taxes today is the best possible course of action.

## TAX-FREE MONEY: LIFE INSURANCE

As previously mentioned, the single greatest tax asset that has come from Congress outside of life insurance is the Roth account. Life insurance is the little known or discussed tax asset that holds some of the greatest value for your financial history both during life and upon death, and it is by far the best tax-advantaged device available. Traditionally, life insurance is viewed as a way to protect your loved ones from financial ruin upon your demise and it should be noted that everyone who cares about someone should have life insurance. By purchasing a life insurance policy, your loved ones will be assured a financial windfall from the life insurance company when you die that will help them with your final expenses and carry on their lives without you comfortably. The best part about the life insurance windfall is the fact that nobody will have to pay tax on the money received. This is the single greatest tax-advantaged device available, but it has one downside, you do not get to use it. Only your heirs will.

The little known and discussed part of life insurance is the cash value build-up within whole life and universal life (permanent) policies. Life insurance is not typically seen as an investment vehicle for building wealth and retirement planning, although it should briefly be discussed why this thought process should be re-evaluated. Permanent life insurance is generally misconceived as something that is very expensive for a wealth accumulation vehicle as there are mortality charges (fees for the death benefit) that detract from the returns that are available and further, those returns do not yield as much as the stock market over the long run. This is why many times you will hear the phrase "buy term and invest the rest," where "term" refers to term insurance.

It's important to review the two terms just used in regard to life insurance: term and permanent. Term insurance is what most people are familiar with. You purchase a certain death benefit that will go to your heirs upon your death and this policy will be in effect for a certain number of years, typically 10 to 20 years. The 10 to 20 years is the term of the policy and once you have reached that end you no longer have insurance unless you purchase another policy at that point.

On the other hand, permanent insurance has no term involved, it is permanent as long as the premiums continue to be paid. Permanent insurance generally has higher premiums than term insurance for the same amount of death benefit coverage and it is this difference that is referred to when people say "invest the rest."

Simply speaking, there are significant differences between these two policies that do not get taken into consideration when providing a comparative analysis in the numbers. One item that gets lost in the fray when comparing term and permanent insurance is that term usually expires before death, in fact insurance studies show less than 1 percent of all term policies pay out death benefit claims. The issue arises when the term expires and the desire to have more insurance is still present. A term policy with the same benefit will be much more expensive than the original policy and, many times, life events occur, such as cancer or heart conditions, which makes it impossible to acquire another policy and leaves your loved ones unprotected and tax-advantaged legacy planning out of the equation.

Another aspect and probably the most important piece in consideration of the future of taxation is the fact that permanent insurance has a cash accumulation value. Two aspects stand out with the cash accumulation value. First, as the cash accumulation value increases the death benefit will also increase whereas term insurance is level. Second, this cash accumulation offers value to you during your lifetime rather than just your heirs upon death. The cash accumulation value can be used for tax-advantaged income during your lifetime through policy loans. Most importantly, this tax-advantaged income is available during retirement for distribution planning, all while offering the same typical financial protection to your heirs.

## TAX-DEFERRED MONEY

Tax-deferred money is the type of money from which most people are familiar, but the idea was also briefly reviewed above. Tax-deferred money is typically your traditional IRA, employer sponsored retirement plan, or a non-qualified annuity. Essentially, money is put into an investment vehicle that will accumulate in value over time and you do not pay taxes on the earnings that grow in these accounts until it is distributed. Taxes must be paid once the money is distributed and, in addition to the taxes, the same negative consequences exist toward additional taxation and expense in other areas as previously discussed.

## TAXABLE MONEY

Taxable money is everything else and is taxable both today and later, whenever it is received.

Of these four types of money, they really come down to two distinct classifications: taxable and tax-advantaged.

The greatest difference when comparing taxable and tax-advantaged income is a function of how much money you will keep after tax. For help in determining what the differences should be, excluding outside factors such as Social Security taxation and AMT, a tax equivalent yield should be used.

## TAX-FREE IN THE REAL WORLD

To put the tax equivalent yield into perspective, consider the following example:

> » Bob and Mary are currently retired and in the 25 percent tax bracket living on Social Security and interest from investments. They have a substantial portion of their investments in municipal bonds yielding 6 percent, which in today's market is quite comforting. The tax equivalent yield they would need to earn from a taxable investment would be 8 percent, a 2 percent gap which seems almost impossible given current market volatility. However, something that has never been put into perspective is that the interest from their municipal bonds is subject to taxation on their Social Security benefits (at 21.25 percent). With this, the yield on their municipal bonds would be 4.725 percent, and the taxable equivalent yield falls to 6.3 percent leaving a gap of only 1.575 percent.

In the end, most people spend their lives accumulating wealth through the best, if not only vehicle they know, a tax-deferred account. This account is most likely a 401(k) or 403(b) plan offered through your employer and may be supplemented with an IRA that was established at one point or another. As the years go by, people blindly throw money into these accounts in an effort to save for a retirement that they someday hope to reach.

The truth is most people have an age selected for when they would like to retire but spend their lives wondering if they will ever be able to actually quit working. To answer this question, you must understand how much money you will have available to contribute toward your needs. In other words, you need to know what your after-tax income will be during this period.

All else being equal, it would not matter if you put your money into a taxable, tax-deferred, or tax-advantaged account as long as income tax rates never change and outside factors are never an event. The net amount you receive in the end will be the same. Unfortunately, this will never be the case. We already know that taxes will increase in the future, meaning we will likely see higher taxes in retirement than during our peak earning years.

Regardless, saving for retirement in any form is a good thing since it appears from all practical perspectives that future government benefits will be cut and taxes will increase. You have the ability to plan today for efficient tax diversification and maximization of your after-tax dollars during your distribution years.

## CHAPTER 13 RECAP //

- Tax-deferred retirement accounts, like traditional IRAs, are subject to future tax rates. You can prepare for future tax rate increases by structuring those assets in tax-advantaged ways.
- Tax-advantaged assets can provide you with non-taxable income during retirement. Roth IRAs, life insurance policies, and municipal bonds are some examples of tax-advantaged money.
- Taking the time to structure assets in tax-advantaged ways can save you thousands of dollars in lower taxes in the future.

# 14
# THE BRANDEIS STORY

Louis Brandeis provides one of the best examples illustrating how tax planning works. Brandeis was Associate Justice on the Supreme Court of the United States from 1916 to 1939. Born in Louisville, Kentucky, Brandeis was an intelligent man with a touch of country charm. He described tax planning this way:

*"I live in Alexandria, Virginia. Near the Court Chambers, there is a toll bridge across the Potomac. When in a rush, I pay the dollar toll and get home early. However, I usually drive outside the downtown section of the city and cross the Potomac on a free bridge.*

*The bridge was placed outside the downtown Washington, D.C. area to serve a useful social service—getting drivers to drive the extra mile and help alleviate congestion during the rush hour.*

*If I went over the toll bridge and through the barrier without paying a toll, I would be committing tax evasion.*

*If I drive the extra mile and drive outside the city of Washington to the free bridge, I am using a legitimate, logical and suitable method of tax avoidance, and I am performing a useful social service by doing so.*

*The tragedy is that **few people know that the free bridge exists.**"*

Like Brandeis, most American taxpayers have options when it comes to "crossing the Potomac," so to speak. It's a financial planner's job to tell you what options are available. You can wait until March to file your taxes, at which time you might pay someone to report and pay the government a larger portion of your income. However, you could instead file before the end of the year, work with your financial professional and incorporate a tax plan as part of your overall financial planning strategy. Filing later is like crossing the toll bridge. Tax planning is like crossing the free bridge.

Which would you rather do?

The answer to this question is easy. Most people want to save money and pay less in taxes. What makes this situation really difficult in real life, however, is that the signs along the side of the road that direct us to the free bridge are not that clear. To normal Americans, and to plenty of people who have studied it, the U.S. tax code is easy to get lost in. There are all kinds of rules, exceptions to rules, caveats and conditions that are difficult to understand, or even to know about. What you really need to know is your options and the bottom line impacts of those options.

## ROTH IRA CONVERSIONS

The attractive qualities of Roth IRAs may have prompted you to explore the possibility of moving some of your assets into a Roth account. Another important difference between the accounts is how they treat Required Minimum Distributions (RMDs). When you turn 70 ½ years old, you are required to take a minimum amount of money out of a traditional IRA. This amount is your RMD. It is treated as taxable income. Roth IRAs, however, do not have RMDs, and their distributions are not taxable. Quite a deal, right?

While having a Roth IRA as part of your portfolio is a good idea, converting assets to a Roth IRA can pose some challenges, depending on what kinds of assets you want to transfer.

One common option is the conversion of a traditional IRA to a Roth IRA. You may have heard about converting your IRA to a Roth IRA, but you might not know the full net result on your income. The main difference between the two accounts is that the growth of investments within a traditional IRA is not taxed until income is withdrawn from the account, whereas taxes are charged on contribution amounts to a Roth IRA, not withdrawals. The problem, however, is that when assets are removed from a traditional IRA, even if the assets are being transferred to a Roth IRA account, taxes apply.

There are a lot of reasons to look at Roth conversions. People have a lot of money in IRAs, up to multiple millions of dollars. Even with $500,000, when they turn 70 ½ years old, their RMD is going to be approximately $18,000, and they have to take that out whether they want to or not. It's a tax issue. Essentially, if you will be subject to high RMDs, it could have impacts on how much of your Social Security is taxable, and on your tax bracket.

By paying taxes now instead of later on assets in a Roth IRA, you can realize tax-advantaged growth. You pay once and you're done paying. Your heirs are done paying. It's a powerful tool. Here's a simple example to show you how powerful it can be:

*Imagine that you pay to convert a traditional IRA to a Roth. You have decided that you want to put the money in a vehicle that gives you a tax-advantaged income option down the road. If you pay a 25 percent tax on that conversion and the Roth IRA then doubles in value over the next 10 years, you could look at your situation as only having paid 12.5 percent tax.*

The prospect of tax-advantaged income is a tempting one. While you have to pay a conversion tax to transfer your assets, you also have turned taxable income into tax free retirement money that you can let grow as long as you want without being required to withdraw it.

There are options, however, that address this problem. Much like the Brandeis story, there may be a "free bridge" option for many investors.

Your financial professional will likely tell you that it is not a matter of whether or not you should perform a Roth IRA conversion, it is a matter of how much you should convert and when.

Here are some of the things to consider before converting to a Roth IRA:

- If you make a conversion before you retire, you may end up paying higher taxes on the conversion because it is likely that you are in some of your highest earning years, placing you in the highest tax bracket of your life. It is possible that a better strategy would be to wait until after you retire, a time when you may have less taxable income, which would place you in a lower tax bracket.
- Many people opt to reduce their work hours from fulltime to part-time in the years before they retire. If you have pursued this option, your income will likely be lower, in turn lowering your tax rate.
- The first years that you draw Social Security benefits can also be years of lower reported income, making it another good time frame in which to convert to a Roth IRA.

One key strategy to handling a Roth IRA conversion is to **always be able to pay the cost of the tax conversion with outside money**. Structuring your tax year to include something like a significant deduction can help you offset the conversion tax. This way you aren't forced to take the money you need for taxes from the value of the IRA. The reason taxes apply to this maneuver is because when you withdraw money from a traditional IRA, it is treated as taxable income by the IRS. Your financial professional, with the help of the CPAs at their firm, may be able to provide you with options like after-tax money, itemized deductions or other situations that can pose effective tax avoidance options.

Some examples of avoiding Roth IRA conversions taxes include:

- *Using medical expenses that are above 10 percent of your Adjusted Gross Income.* If you have health care costs that you can list as itemized deductions, you can convert an amount of income from a traditional IRA to a Roth IRA that is offset by the deductible amount. Essentially, deductible medical expenses negate the taxes resulting from recording the conversion.

- *Individuals, usually small business owners, who are dealing with a Net Operating Loss (NOL).* If you have NOLs, but aren't able to utilize all of them on your tax return, you can carry them forward to offset the taxable income from the taxes on income you convert to a Roth IRA.

- *Charitable giving.* If you are charitably inclined, you can use the amount of your donations to reduce the amount of taxable income you have during that year. By matching the amount you convert to a Roth IRA to the amount your taxable income was reduced by charitable giving, you can essentially avoid taxation on the conversion. You may decide to double your donations to a charity in one year, giving them two years' worth of donations in order to offset the Roth IRA conversion tax on this year's tax return.

- *Investments that are subject to depletion.* Certain investments can kick off depletion expenses. If you make an investment and are subject to depletion expenses, they can be deducted and used to offset a Roth IRA conversion tax.

Not all of the above scenarios work for everyone, and there are many other options for offsetting conversion taxes. The point is that you have options, and your financial professional and tax professional can help you understand those options.

If you have a traditional IRA, Roth conversions are something you should look at. As you approach retirement you should consider your options and make choices that keep more of your money in your pocket, not the government's.

## ADDITIONAL TAX BENEFITS OF ROTH IRAS

Not only do Roth IRAs provide you with tax-advantaged growth, they also give you a tax diversified landscape that allows you to maximize your distributions. Chances are that no matter the circumstances, you will have taxed income and other assets subject to taxation. *But if you have a Roth IRA, you have the unique ability to manage your Adjusted Gross Income (AGI), because you have a tax-advantaged income option!*

Converting to a Roth IRA can also help you preserve and build your legacy. Because Roth IRAs are exempt from RMDs, after you make a conversion from a traditional IRA, your Roth account can grow tax-advantaged for another 15, 20 or 25 years and it can be used as tax-advantaged income by your heirs. It is important to note, however, that non-spousal beneficiaries do have to take RMDs from a Roth IRA, or choose to stretch it and draw tax-advantaged income out of it over their lifetime.

## TO CONVERT OR NOT TO CONVERT?

Conversions aren't only for retirees. You can convert at any time. Your choice should be based on your individual circumstances and tax situation. Sticking with a traditional IRA or converting to a Roth, again, depends on your individual circumstances, including your income, your tax bracket and the amount of deductions you have each year.

Is it better to have a Roth IRA or traditional IRA? It depends on your individual circumstance. Some people don't mind having taxable income from an IRA. Their income might not be very high and their RMD might not bump their tax bracket up, so it's not as big a deal. A similar situation might involve income from Social Security. Social Security benefits are taxed based on other income you are drawing. If you are in a position where none or very little of your Social Security benefit is subject to taxes, paying income tax on your RMD may be very easy.

> » *There are also situations where leveraging taxable income from a traditional IRA can work to your advantage come tax time. For example, Darrel and Linda dream of buying a boat when they retire. It is something they have looked forward to their entire marriage. In addition to the savings and investments that they created to supply them with income during retirement, which includes a traditional IRA, they have also saved money for the sole purpose of purchasing a boat once they stop working.*
>
> *When the time comes and they finally buy the boat of their dreams, they pay an additional $15,000 in sales taxes that year because of the large purchase. Because they are retired and earning less money, the deductions they used to be able to realize from their income taxes are no longer there. The high amount of sales taxes they paid on the boat puts them in a*

*position where they could benefit from taking taxable income from a traditional IRA.*

*When Darrel and Linda's financial professional learns about their purchase, he immediately contacts a CPA at his firm to run the numbers. They determine that by taking a $15,000 distribution from their IRA, they could fulfill their income needs to offset the $15,000 sales tax deduction that they were claiming due to the purchase of their boat. In the end, they pay zero taxes on their income distribution from their IRA.*

The moral of the story? ***Having a tax diversified landscape gives you options.*** Having capital assets that can be liquidated, tax-advantaged income options and sources that can create capital gains or capital losses will put you in a position to play your cards right no matter what you want to accomplish with your taxes. The ace up your sleeve is your financial professional and the CPAs they work with. Do yourself a favor and *plan* your taxes instead of *reporting* them!

## CHAPTER 14 RECAP //

- Converting a traditional IRA to a Roth IRA can help you avoid paying a higher tax rate in the future, and let you take advantage of paying your taxes while in a lower tax bracket.
- You make more money by saving on taxes than you do by making more money. This simple concept becomes extremely valuable to people in retirement and those living on fixed incomes.
- When you report your taxes, you are paying to record history. When you *plan* your taxes with a financial professional, you are proactively finding the best options for your tax return.
- No one knows what the future of U.S taxation holds. Today's tax rate and landscape is known, but tomorrow's isn't. The only thing that seems likely is the trend of increasing taxation.
- Look for the "free bridge" option in your tax strategy.
- Converting from a traditional to a Roth IRA can provide you with tax-advantaged retirement income.
- Converting to a Roth IRA can also help you preserve and build your legacy.
- There are many ways to reduce your taxes. Being smart about your Roth IRA conversion is one of the main ways to do so.

# 15
# PREPARING YOUR LEGACY

*You don't buy life insurance for yourself:*
*you buy it for your loved ones.*

Many retired people may feel like life insurance is less relevant for them at their stage in life. With the kids grown, you may think being insured isn't necessary. The opposite may be true, however. If you recall the previous discussion of spousal continuation, you'll remember than the loss of a spouse can result in a 40 percent loss of household income. Making up for that loss during retirement, when you aren't working and receiving a paycheck or aggressively investing, can be challenging at best or impossible at worst. Instead of going back to work, selling your assets or borrowing, you may be able to rely on an insurance policy that meets your needs.

You or your spouse cannot be replaced, but the income loss one of you leaves behind can be. Relying on life insurance for that safety net can be a wise and affordable option. If you take steps while you are young enough and healthy enough to get a beneficial policy, a life insurance policy can replace income and help cover potential long-term care costs.

Additionally, you may choose to use life insurance to plan for funding your grandchildren's education, contributing to your legacy (tax-free!), or redirecting RMDs from an IRA into a tax-advantaged account. If you have a substantial IRA and don't need to access it for income, you can save yourself and your beneficiaries the burden of taxation by transferring it to a life insurance policy.

## BUILDING YOUR LEGACY WITH LIFE INSURANCE

There are many unique benefits of life insurance that can help your beneficiaries get the most out of your legacy. Some of them include:

- Providing beneficiaries with a tax-free, liquid asset.
- Covering the costs associated with your death.
- Providing income for your dependents.
- Offering an investment opportunity for your beneficiaries.
- Covering expenses such as tuition or mortgage down payments for your children or grandchildren.

Very few people want life insurance, but nearly everyone wants what it does. Life insurance is specifically, and uniquely, capable of creating money when it is needed most. When a loved one passes, no amount of money can remove the pain of loss. And certainly, money doesn't solve the challenges that might arise with losing someone important.

It has been said that when you have money, you have options. When you don't have money, your options are severely limited. You might imagine a life insurance policy can give your family and loved ones options that would otherwise be impossible.

» *Paul spent the last 20 years building a small business. In so many ways, it is a family business. Each of his three children, Katy, Cheryl and Mike, worked in the shop part-time during high school. But after all three attended college, only Katy returned to join her father, and eventually will run the business full-time when Paul retires.*

*Paul is able to retire comfortably on Social Security and on-going income from the shop, but the business is nearly his entire financial legacy. It is his wish that Katy own the business outright, but he also wants to leave an equal legacy to each of his three children.*

*There is no simple way to divide the business into thirds and still leave the business intact for Katy.*

*Paul ends up buying a life insurance policy to make up the difference. Cheryl and Mike will receive their share of an inheritance in cash from the life insurance policy and Katy will be able to inherit the business intact.*

*Paul is able to accomplish his goals, treat all three children equitably and leave Katy the business she helped to build.*

If you have a life insurance policy but you haven't looked at it in a while, you may not know how it operates, how much it is worth and how it will be distributed to your beneficiaries. You may also need to update your beneficiaries on your policy. In short, without a comprehensive review of your policy, you don't really know where the money will go or to whom it will go.

If you don't have a life insurance policy but are looking for options to maintain and grow your legacy, speaking with a professional can show you the benefits of life insurance. Many people don't consider buying a life insurance policy until some event in their life triggers it, like the loss of a loved one, an accident or a health condition.

## BENEFITS OF LIFE INSURANCE

Life insurance is a useful and secure tool for contingency planning, ensuring that your dependents receive the assets that you want them to have, and for meeting the financial goals you have set for the future. While it bears the name "Life Insurance," it is, in reality, a diverse financial tool that can meet many needs. The main function of a life insurance policy is to provide financial assets for your survivors. Life insurance is particularly efficient at achieving this goal because it provides a tax-advantaged lump sum of money in the form of a death benefit to your beneficiary or beneficiaries. That financial asset can be used in a number of ways. It can be structured as an investment to provide income for your spouse or children, it can pay down debts, and it can be used to cover estate taxes and other costs associated with death.

Tax liabilities on the estate you leave behind are inevitable. Capital property, for instance, is taxed at its fair market value at the time of your death, unless that property is transferred to your spouse. If the property has appreciated during the time you owned it, taxation on capital gains will occur. Registered Retirement Savings Plans (RRSPs) and other similarly structured assets are also included as taxable income unless transferred to a beneficiary as well. Those are just a few examples of how an estate can become subject to a heavy tax burden. The unique benefits of a life insurance policy provide ways to handle this tax burden, solving any liquidity problems that may arise if your family members want to hold onto an illiquid asset, such as a piece of property or an investment. Life insurance can provide a significant amount of money to a family member or other beneficiary, and that money is likely to remain exempt from taxation or seizure.

One of life insurance's most important benefits is that it is not considered part of the estate of the policy holder. The death benefit that is paid by the insurance company goes exclusively to the beneficiaries listed on the policy. This shields the proceeds of the policy from fees and costs that can reduce an estate, including probate proceedings, attorneys' fees and claims made by creditors. The distribution of your life insurance policy is also unaffected by delays of the estate's distribution, like probate. Your beneficiaries will get the proceeds of the policy in a timely fashion, regardless of how long it takes for the rest of your estate to be settled.

Investing a portion of your assets in a life insurance policy can also protect that portion of your estate from creditors. If you owe money to someone or some entity at the time of your death, a creditor is not able to claim any money from a life insurance policy or an annuity, for that matter. An exception to this rule is if you had already used the life insurance policy as collateral against a loan. If a large portion of the money you want to dedicate to your legacy is sitting in a savings account, investment or other liquid form, creditors may be able to receive their claim on it before your beneficiaries get anything that is if there's anything left. A life insurance policy protects your assets from creditors and ensures that your beneficiaries get the money that you intend them to have.

## HOW MUCH LIFE INSURANCE DO YOU NEED?

Determining the type of policy and the amount right for you depends on an analysis of your needs. A financial professional can help you complete a needs analysis that will highlight the amount of insurance that you require to meet your goals. This type of personalized review will allow you to determine ways to continue providing income for your spouse or any dependents you may have. A financial professional can also help you calculate the amount of income that your policy should replace to meet the needs of your beneficiaries and the duration of the distribution of that income.

You may also want to use your life insurance policy to meet any expenses associated with your death. These can include funeral costs, fees from probate and legal proceedings, and taxes. You may also want to dedicate a portion of your policy proceeds to help fund tuition or other expenses for your children or grandchildren. You can buy a policy and hope it covers all of those costs, or you can work with a professional who can calculate exactly how much insurance you need and how to structure it to meet your goals. Which would you rather do?

## AVOIDING POTENTIAL SNAGS

There are benefits to having life insurance supersede the direction given in a will or other legacy plan, but there are also some potential snags that you should address to meet your wishes. For example, if your will instructs that your assets be divided equally between your two children but your life insurance beneficiary is listed as just one of the children, the assets in the life insurance policy will only be distributed to the child listed as the beneficiary. The beneficiary designation of your life insurance supersedes your will's instruction. This is important to understand when designating beneficiaries on a policy you purchase. Work with a professional to make sure that your beneficiaries are accurately listed on your assets, especially your life insurance policies.

## USING LIFE INSURANCE TO BUILD YOUR LEGACY

Depending on your goals, there are strategies you can use that could multiply how much you leave behind. Life insurance is one of the most surefire and efficient investment tools for building a substantial legacy that will meet your financial goals.

Here is a brief overview of how life insurance can boost your legacy:

- Life insurance provides an immediate increase in your legacy.
- It provides an income tax-advantaged death benefit for your beneficiaries.

- A good life insurance policy has the opportunity to accumulate value over time.
- It may have an option to include long-term care (LTC) or chronic illness benefits should you require them.

If your Green Money income needs for retirement are met and you have Yellow Money assets that will provide for your future expenses, you may have extra assets that you want to earmark as legacy funds. By electing to invest those assets into a life insurance policy, you can immediately increase the amount of your legacy. Remember, **life insurance allows you to transfer a tax-advantaged lump sum of money to your beneficiaries. It remains in your control during your lifetime, can provide for your long-term care needs and bypasses probate costs.** And make no mistake, taxes can have a huge impact on your legacy. Not only that, income and assets from your legacy can have tax implications for your beneficiaries, as well.

Here's a brief overview of how taxes could affect your legacy and your beneficiaries:

- The higher your income, the higher the rate at which it is taxed.
- Withdrawals from qualified plans are taxed as income.
- What's more, when you leave a large qualified plan, it ends up being taxed at a high rate.
- If you left a $500,000 IRA to your child, they could end up owing as much as $140,000 in income taxes.
- However, if you could just withdraw $50,000 a year, the tax bill might only be $10,000 per year.

How could you use that annual amount to leave a larger legacy? Luckily, you can leverage a life insurance policy to avoid those tax penalties, preserving a larger amount of your legacy and freeing your beneficiaries from an added tax burden.

» *When Brenda turned 70 years old, she decided it was time to look into life insurance policy options. She still feels young, but she remembers that her mother died in early 70s, and she wants to plan ahead so she can pass on some of her legacy to her grandchildren just like her grandmother did for her.*

*Brenda doesn't really want to think about life insurance, but she does want the security, reliability and tax-advantaged distribution that it offers. She lives modestly, and her Social Security benefit meets most of her income needs. As the beneficiary of her late husband's Certificate of Deposit (CD), she has $100,000 in an account that she has never used and doesn't anticipate ever needing since her income needs were already met.*

*After looking at several different investment options with a professional, Brenda decides that a Single Premium life insurance policy fits her needs best. She can buy the policy with a $100,000 one-time payment and she is guaranteed that it would provide more than the value of the contract to her beneficiaries. If she left the money in the CD, it would be subject to taxes. But for every dollar that she puts into the life insurance policy, her beneficiaries are guaranteed at least that dollar plus a death benefit, and all of it will be **tax-free!***

*For $100,000, Brenda's particular policy offers a $170,000 death benefit distribution to her beneficiaries. By moving the $100,000 from a CD to a life insurance policy, Brenda increases her legacy by 70 percent. Not only that, she has also sheltered it from taxes, so her beneficiaries will be able to receive $1.70 for every $1.00 that she entered into the policy! While buying the policy doesn't allow her to use the money for herself, it does allow her family to benefit from her well-planned legacy.*

## MAKE YOUR WISHES KNOWN

Estate taxes used to be a much hotter topic in the mid-2000s when the estate tax limits and exclusions were much smaller and taxed at a higher rate than today. In 2008, estates valued at $2 million or more were taxed at 45 percent. Just two years later, the limit was raised to $5 million dollars taxed at 35 percent. The limit has continued to rise ever since. The limit applies to fewer people than before. Estate organization, however, is just as important as ever, and it affects everyone.

Ask yourself:

- Are your assets actually titled and held the way you think they are?
- Are your beneficiaries set up the way you think they should be?
- Have there been changes to your family or those you desire as beneficiaries?

There is more to your legacy beyond your property, money, investments and other assets that you leave to family members, loved ones and charities. Everyone has a legacy beyond money. You also leave behind personal items of importance, your values and beliefs, your personal and family history, and your wishes. Beyond a will and a plan for your assets, it is important that you make your wishes known to someone for the rest of your personal legacy. When it comes time for your family and loved ones to make decisions after you are gone, knowing your wishes can help them make decisions that honor you and your legacy, and give meaning to what you leave behind. Your professional can help you organize.

Think about your:

- Personal stories / recollections
- Values
- Personal items of emotional significance

- Financial assets

Do you want to make a plan to pass these things on to your family?

## WORKING WITH A PROFESSIONAL

Part of using life insurance to your greatest advantage is selecting the policy and provider that can best meet your goals. Venturing into the jungle of policies, brokers and salespeople can be overwhelming, and can leave you wondering if you've made the best decision. Working with a trusted financial professional can help you cut through the red tape, the "sales-speak" and confusion to find a policy that meets your goals and best serves your desires for your money. If you already have a policy, a financial professional can help you review it and become familiar with the policy's premium, the guarantees the policy affords, its performance, and its features and benefits. A financial professional can also help you make any necessary changes to the policy.

> » When Sofia turned 88, her daughter finally convinced her to meet with a financial professional to help her organize her assets and get her legacy in order. Although Sofia is reluctant to let a stranger in on her personal finances, she ends up very glad that she did.
>
> In the process of listing Sofia's assets and her beneficiaries, her professional finds a man's name listed as the beneficiary of an old life insurance annuity that she owns. It turns out, the man is Sofia's ex-husband who is still alive. Had Sofia passed away before her ex-husband, the annuities and any death benefits that came with them, would have been passed on to her ex-husband. This does not reflect her latest wishes.

Things change, relationships evolve and the way you would like your legacy organized needs to adapt to the changes that happen throughout your life. There may be a new child or grandchild in your family, or you may have been divorced or remarried. A professional will regularly review your legacy assets and ask you questions to make sure that everything is up to date and that the current organization reflects your current wishes.

## CHAPTER 15 RECAP //

- You can structure your assets in ways that maximize distributions to your beneficiaries.
- Working with a financial professional can help ensure that many of your assets avoid the ponderous and expensive probate process.
- A financial professional can help review the details of the assets you have designated to be a part of your legacy and make sure that you aren't unintentionally disinheriting your heirs.
- Life insurance provides the distribution of tax-free, liquid assets to your beneficiaries.
- Investing in a life insurance policy can significantly build your legacy.
- Organizing your legacy will allow you to make sure your wishes are properly carried through.
- You can take advantage of a "Stretch IRA" to provide income for you, your spouse and your beneficiaries throughout their lifetimes.
- Understand if your assets will be distributed *per stirpes* or *per capita*.
- Working with a financial professional can help you select the policy that best meets your needs, or can help you fine tune your existing policy to better reflect your desires and intentions.

# 16
# HOW TO CHOOSE A FINANCIAL PROFESSIONAL

*Find a planner you can trust.*

From the moment you dip your toes into the retirement planning pool to the point you start swimming laps, your assets organized, your income needs met, and your accumulation and legacy plans in place, working with a professional that you trust can make all the difference in how well your retirement reflects your desires.

It is important to know what you are looking for before taking the plunge. There are many people that would love to handle your money, but not everyone is qualified to handle it in a way that leads to a holistic approach to creating a solid retirement plan.

The distinction being made here is that you should look for someone that puts your interests first and actively wants to help you meet your goals and objectives. Oftentimes, the products someone sells you matter less than their dedication to making sure that you have a plan that meets your needs.

Professionals take your whole financial position into consideration. They make plans that adjust your risk exposure, invest in tools that secure your desired income during retirement and create investment strategies that allow you to continue accumulating wealth during your retirement for you to use later or to contribute to your legacy. If you buy stocks with a broker, use a different agent for a life insurance policy and have an unmanaged 401(k) through your employer, working with a financial professional will consolidate the management of your assets so you have one trustworthy person quarterbacking all of the team elements of your portfolio. Financial products and investment tools change, but the concepts that lie behind wise retirement planning are lasting. In the end, a financial professional's approach is designed for those serious about planning for retirement. *Can you say the same thing about the person that advises you about your financial life?*

It's easy to see how choosing a financial professional can be one of the most important decisions you can make in your life. Not only do they provide you with advice, they also manage the personal assets that supply your retirement income and contribute to your legacy. So, how do you find a good one?

## HOW TO FIND A FINANCIAL PROFESSIONAL YOU CAN TRUST

Taking care to select a financial professional is one of the best things you can do for yourself and for your future. Your professional has influence and control of your investment decisions, making their role in your life more than just important. Your financial security and the quality of your retirement depends on the decisions, investment strategies and asset structuring that you and your professional create.

Working with a professional is different than calling up a broker when you want to buy or trade some stock. This isn't a decision that you can hand off to anyone else. You need to bring your time and attention to the table when it comes to finding someone with whom you can entrust your financial life. Separating the wheat from the chaff will take some work, but you'll be happy you did it.

While no one can tell you exactly who to choose or how to choose them, the following information can help you narrow the field:

- You can start by asking your friends, family and colleagues for referrals. You will want to pay particular attention to the recommendations that you get from others who are in your similar financial situation and who have similar lifestyle choices. The professional for the CEO of your company may have a different skill-set than the skill-set of the professional befitting your cousin who has three kids and a Subaru like you. Do follow-up research on the internet as well. Look up the people who have been recommended to you on websites like LinkedIn that show the work history, referrals and experience of the candidates that you find most attractive. You will also learn about the firms with or for whom they work. The investment philosophies and reputations of the companies they work for will tell you a lot about how they will handle your money.

- The other side of the coin, however, is that everyone and their brother has a recommendation about how you should manage your money and who should manage it for you. From hot stock tips to "the best money manager in the state," people love to share good information that makes them look like they are in-the-know. Nobody wants to talk about the bad stock purchases they made, the times they lost money and the poor selections they made regarding financial professionals or stock brokers. If you decide to take a friend or family member's recommendation, make sure they have a substantial, long-term experience with the financial professional and that their glowing review isn't just based on a one-time "win."

- It is important to understand how your professional is being paid. It is generally considered preferable to work with a fee-based professional who will not have conflicts of interests between earning a commission and acting in your best interests.

- Many professionals may also be brokers or dealers that can earn commissions on things like life insurance, certain types of annuities and disability insurance. These professionals have most likely intentionally overlapped their roles so that if their clients choose to purchase insurance or investment products that require a broker or dealer, those clients won't have to find an additional person to work with. Again, understanding the role of your professional will help you make your determination.

## NARROWING THE FIELD

**1. Decide on the Type of Professional with Whom You Want to Work.** There are four basic kinds of financial professionals. Many professionals may play overlapping roles. It is important to know a professional's primary function, how they charge for their services and whether they are obligated to act in your best interest.

*Registered representatives*, better known as stockbrokers or bank / investment representatives, make their living by earning commissions on insurance products and investment services. Stockbrokers basically sell you things. The products from which they make the highest commission are sometimes the products that they recommend to their clients. If you want to make a simple transaction, such as buying or selling a particular stock, a registered representative can help you. Although registered representatives are licensed professionals, if you want to create a structured and planful approach to positioning your assets for retirement, you might want to consider continuing your search.

The term "planner" is often misused. It can refer to credible professionals that are CPAs, CFPs and ChFCs to your uncle's next door neighbor who claims to have a lead on some undervalued stock about to be "discovered." A wide array of people may claim to be planners because there are no requirements to be a planner. The term financial planner, however, refers to someone who is properly registered as an investment advisor representative and serves as a fiduciary as described below.

Investment advisor representatives are the diamonds in the rough. They are compensated on a fee basis, but some may also be licensed as stockbrokers or insurance agents, which allows them to earn commissions on certain transactions. More importantly, **investment advisor representatives are financial fiduciaries, meaning they are required to make financial decisions in your best interest and reflecting your risk tolerance.** Investment advisor representatives are held to high ethical standards and are highly regarded in the financial industry. Investment advisor representatives also often take a more comprehensive approach to asset management. These professionals are trained and credentialed to plan and coordinate their clients' assets in order to meet their goals or retirement and legacy planning. They are not focused on individual stocks, investments or markets. They look at the big picture, the whole enchilada.

*Money managers* are on par with investment advisor representatives. However, they are often given explicit permission to make investment decisions without advanced approval by their clients.

Understanding who you are working with and what their title is the first step to planning your retirement. While each of the above-mentioned types of financial professionals can help you with aspects of your finances, investment advisor representatives have the most intimate role, the most objective investment strategies and the most unbiased mode of compensation for their services. An investment advisor representative can also help you with the non-financial aspects of your legacy and can help you find ways to create a tax planning strategy to help you save money.

**2. Be Objective.** At the end of the day, you need to separate the weak from the strong. While you might want a strong personal rapport with your professional, or you may want to choose your professional for their personality and positive attitude, it is more important that you find someone who will give sage advice regarding achieving your retirement goals.

It can be helpful to use a process of elimination to narrow the field of potential professionals. Look into five or six potential leads and cross off your list the ones that don't meet your requirements until only one or two remain. Cross-check your remaining choices against the list of things you need from a professional. Make sure they represent a firm that has the investment tools and products that you desire, and make sure they have experience in retirement planning. That is, after all, the main goal.

Don't be afraid to investigate each of your candidates. You'll want to ask the same questions and look for the same information from everyone you consider so you can then compare them and discern which is best for you. You'll want to take a look at the specific credentials of each professional, their experience and competence, their ethics and fiduciary status, their history and track record, and a list of the services that they offer. The professionals who meet all or most of your qualifications are the ones you will contact for an interview.

Potential professionals should meet your qualifications in the following categories:

- *Credentials:* Look at their experience, the quality of their education, any associations to which they belong and certifications they have earned. Someone who has continued their professional education through ongoing certifications will be more up-to-date on current financial practices compared to someone who got their degree 25 years ago and hasn't done a thing since.
- *Practices:* Look at the track record of your candidates, how they are compensated for their services, the reports and analysis they offer, and their value added services.
- *Services:* Your professional must meet your needs. If you are planning your retirement, you should work with someone who offers services that help you to that end. You want someone who can offer planning, advice on investment strategies, ways to calculate risk, advice on insurance and annuities products, and ways to manage your tax strategy.
- *Ethics:* You want to work with someone who is above board and does things the right way. Vet them by checking their compliance record, current licensing, fiduciary status and, yes, even their criminal record. You never know!

**3. Ask for and Check References.** Once you have selected two or three professionals that you want to meet, call or email them and ask for references. Every professional should be able to provide you with at least two or three names. In fact, they will probably be eager to share them with you. Most professionals rely on references for validation of their success, quality of services and likability. You should, however, take them with a grain of salt. You have no way to know whether or not references are a professional's friends or colleagues.

It is worth contacting references, however, to check for inconsistencies. Ask each reference the same set of questions to get the same basic information. How long have they been working with the professional? What kind of services have they used and were they happy with them? What type of financial planning did they use the professional for? Were they versed in the type of financial planning that you needed? You can also ask them direct questions to elicit candid responses. What was the full cost of the expenses that your professional charged you? Do the reports and statements you receive come from the same firm? Questions like these can help you get a sense of how well the reference knows their professional and whether or not they are a quality reference.

A good reference is a bit like icing on the cake. It's nice to have them, but nothing speaks louder than a good track record and quality experience. And remember that a good reference, while nice to hear, is relatively cheap. How many times have you heard someone on the golf course or at work telling you how great their stockbroker is? But how many times have you heard about the bad investments or losses they have experienced?

**4. Use the Internet.** As a final step before picking up the phone and calling your candidates, do some digging to discover if anyone on your list has a history of unlawful or unethical practices, or has been disciplined for any of their professional behavior or decisions. Don't worry, you don't have to hire a private investigator. You can easily find this information on the Financial Industry Regulatory Authority's (FINRA) online BrokerCheck tool: http://www.finra.org/Investors/ToolsCalculators/BrokerCheck/.

You should obviously explore the website of a potential professional and the website of the firm that they represent. The internet allows you to go beyond the online business card of a professional to gain access to information that they don't control. It may all be good information! Or a brief search of the internet could reveal a sketchy past. The best part is that the internet allows you to find helpful information in an anonymous fashion.

Start with Google (www.google.com) and search the name of a potential professional and their firm. Keep your eyes trained on third party sources such as articles, blog posts or news stories that mention the professional. You can also check a professional's compliance records online with the Financial Industry Regulatory Authority (FINRA) and the Securities and Exchange Commission (SEC). If you want to dig deeper, you can combine search terms like "scams," "lawsuits," "suspensions" and "fraud" with a professional's or firm's name to see what information arises. More likely than not, you won't find anything. But if you do, you'll be glad that you checked.

## HOW TO INTERVIEW CANDIDATES

After vetting your candidates and narrowing down a list of professionals that you think might be a good fit for you, it's time to start interviewing.

When you meet in person with a professional, you want to take advantage of your time with them. The presentations and information that they share with you will be important to pay attention to, but you will also want to control some aspects of the interview. After a professional has told you what they want you to hear, it's time to ask your own questions to get the specific information you need to make your decision.

Make sure to prepare a list of questions and an informal agenda so that you can keep track of what you want to ask and what points you want the professional to touch on during the interview. Using the same questions and agenda will also allow you to more easily compare the professionals after you have interviewed them all. Remember that these interviews are just that, *interviews*. You are meeting with several professionals to determine with whom you want to work. Don't agree to anything or sign anything during an interview until after you have made your final decision.

It can also be helpful to put a time limit on your interviews and to meet the professionals at their offices. The time limit will keep things on track and will allow structured time for presentations and questions/discussion. By meeting them at their office, you can get a sense of the work environment, the staff culture and attitude, and how the firm does business. If you are unable to travel to a professional's office and must meet them at your home or office, make sure that your interviews are scheduled with plenty of time between so the professionals don't cross each other's paths.

You can use the following questions during an initial interview to get an understanding of how each professional does business and whether they are a good fit for you:

**1. How do you charge for your services? How much do you charge?** This information should be easy to find on their website, but if you don't see it, ask. Find out if they charge an initial planning fee, if they charge a percentage for assets under their management and if they make money by selling specific financial products or services. If so, you should follow up by asking how much the service costs. This will give you an idea of how they really make their money and if they have incentive to sell certain products over others. Make sure you understand exactly how you will be charged so there are no surprises down the road if you decide to work with this person.

**2. What are your credentials, licenses, and certifications?** There are Certified Financial Planners (CFPs), Chartered Financial Consultants (ChFCs), Investment Advisor Representatives, Certified Public Accountants (CPAs) and Personal Financial Specialists (PFSs). Whatever their credentials or titles, you want to be sure that the professional you work with is an expert in the field relevant to your circumstances. If you want someone to manage your money, you will most likely look for an Investment Advisor.

Someone that works with an independent firm will likely have a team of CPAs, CFPs and other financial experts upon whom they can draw. If you like the professional you are meeting with and you think they might be a good fit, but they don't have the accounting experience you want them to have, ask about their firm and the resources available to them. If they work closely with CPAs that are experienced in your needs, it could be a good match.

**3. What are the financial services that you and your firm provide?** The question within the question here is, "Can you help me achieve my goals?" Some people can only provide you with investment advice, and others are tax consultants. You will likely want to work with someone that provides a complete suite of financial planning services and products that touch on retirement planning, insurance options, legacy structuring, and tax planning. Whatever services they provide, make sure they meet your needs and your anticipated needs.

**4. What kinds of clients do you work with the most?** A lot of financial professionals work within a niche: retirement planning, risk assessment, life insurance, etc. Finding someone who works with other people that are in the same financial boat as you and who have similar goals can be an important way to make sure they understand your needs. While someone might be a crackerjack annuities cowboy, you might not be interested in that option. Ask follow-up questions that will really help you understand where their expertise lies and whether or not their experience lines up with your needs.

**5. May I see a sample of one of your financial plans?** You wouldn't buy a car without test driving it, and you should not work with a professional without seeing a sample of how they do business. While there is no formal structure that a financial plan has to follow, the variation between professionals can help you find someone who "speaks your language." One professional may provide you with an in-depth analysis that relies heavily on info graphics and diagrams. Someone else may give you a seven page review of your assets and general recommendations. By seeing a sample plan, you can narrow down who presents information in the way that you desire and in ways that you understand.

**6. How do you approach investing?** You may be entirely in the dark about how to approach your investments, or you might have some guiding principles. Either way, ask each candidate what their philosophy is. Some will resonate with you and some won't. A good professional who has a realistic approach to investing won't promise you the moon or tell you that they can make you a lot of money. Professionals who are successful at retirement planning and full service financial management will tell you that they will listen to your goals, risk tolerance and comfort level with different types of investment strategies. Working with someone that you trust is critical, and this question in particular can help you find out who you can and who you can't.

**7. How do you remain in contact with your clients?** Does your prospective professional hold annual, quarterly or monthly meetings? How often do *you* want to meet with your professional? Some people want to check in once a year, go over everything and make sure their ducks are all in a row. If any changes over the previous year or additions to their legacy planning strategy came up, they'll do it on that date. Other people want a monthly update to be more involved in the decision making process and to understand what's happening with their portfolio. You basically need to determine the right degree of involvement for both you and your financial professional. You'll also want to feel out how your professional communicates. Do you prefer phone calls or face-to-face meetings? Do you want your professional to explain things to you in detail or to summarize for you what decisions they've made? Is the professional willing to give you their direct phone number or their email address? More importantly, do you want that information and do you want to be able to contact them in those ways?

**8. Are you my main contact, or do you work with a team?** This is another way of finding out how involved with you your professional will be, and how often they will meet with you. It is also a way to discover how the firm they represent operates and manages their clients. Some professionals will answer their own phone, meet with you regularly and have your home phone number on speed dial. Others will meet with you once a year and have a partner or assistant check in with you every quarter to give you an update. Other companies take an entirely team-based approach whereby clients have a main contact but their portfolio is handled by a team of professionals that represent the firm. One way isn't better than another, but one way will be best for you. Find out how the professional you are interviewing operates before entering into an agreement.

**9. How do you provide a unique experience for your clients?** This is a polite way of asking, "Why should I work with you?" A professional should have a compelling answer to this question that connects with you. Their answer will likely touch on their investment philosophy, their communication style and their expertise. If you hear them describing strengths and philosophies that resonate with you, keep them on your list. Some professionals will tell you that they will make investments with your money that match your values, others will say they will maximize your returns and others will say they will protect your capital while structuring your assets for income. Whatever you're looking for in a professional, you will most likely find it in the answer to this question.

This last question you will want to ask *yourself* after you've met with someone who you are considering hiring:

**10. Did they ask questions and show signs that they were interested in working with me?** A professional who will structure your assets to reflect your risk tolerance and to position you for a comfortable retirement must be a good listener. You will want to pass by a professional who talks non-stop and tells you what to do without listening to what you want them to do. If you felt they listened well and understood your needs, and seemed interested and experienced in your situation, then they might be right for you.

## THE IMPORTANCE OF INDEPENDENCE

Not all investment firms and financial professionals are created equal. The information in this book has systematically shown that leveraging investments for income and accumulation in today's market requires new ideas and modern planning. In short, you need innovative ideas to come up with the creative solutions that will provide you with the retirement that you want. Innovation thrives on independence. No matter how good a financial professional is, the firm that they represent needs to operate on principles that make sense in today's economy. Remember, advice about money has been around forever. Good advice, however, changes with the times.

Timing the market, relying on the sale of stocks for income and banking on high treasury and bond returns are not strategies. They aren't even realistic ways to make money or to generate income. Working with an independent agent can help you break free from the old ways of thinking and position you to create a realistic retirement plan.

Working with an independent professional who relies on fee-based income tied to the success of their performance will also give you greater peace of mind. When you do well, they do well, and that's the way it should be. Your independent financial professional will make sure that:

- Your assets are organized and structured to reflect your risk tolerance.
- Your assets will be available to you when you need them and in the way that you need them.
- You will have a lifetime income that will support your lifestyle through your retirement.
- You are handling your taxes as efficiently as possible.
- Your legacy is in order.
- Your Red Money is turned into Yellow Money, and is managed in your best interest.

*» Remember Becky and Jim from Chapter 2? Even though they knew they had Social Security benefits coming, they placed some money in savings and each had a pension or a 401(k).* **Before they met with a financial professional, they had no idea what their retirement would look like.** *After they met with an agent, they knew exactly what types of assets they had, how much they were worth, how much risk they were exposed to and how they were going to be distributed. They also created an income plan so that they could pay their bills every month the moment they retired, and they maximized their Social Security benefit by targeting the year and month they would get the most lifetime benefits. After their income needs were met, they were able to continue accumulating wealth by investing their extra assets to serve them in the future and contribute to their legacy. Their professional also helped them*

*make decisions that impacted their taxes, protecting the value of their assets and allowing them to keep more of their money.*

*This isn't a fairy tale scenario. This is an example of how much you stand to gain by meeting with a financial professional who can help you create a planful approach to your retirement. The concept of Know So and Hope So didn't just apply to their money.. They* **hoped** *that they would have enough for retirement and that they had worked hard enough and saved enough to maintain their lifestyle. Working with a financial professional allowed them to* **know** *that their income needs were secured and structured to provide them with income for the rest of their lives and with some money to spare.*

*Now, ask yourself: Is your retirement built on hopes and dreams, or a solid, predictable plan?*

## IT'S WORTH IT!

Finding, interviewing and selecting a financial professional can seem like a daunting task. And honestly, it will take a good amount of work to narrow the field and find the one you want. In the end, it is worth the blood, sweat and tears. Your retirement, lifestyle, assets and legacy is on the line. The choices you make today will have lasting impacts on your life and the life of your loved ones. Working with someone you trust and know you can rely on to make decisions that will benefit you is invaluable. The work it takes to find them is something you will never regret.

Here is a recap of why working with a financial professional is the best retirement decision you can make:

## CHAPTER 16 RECAP //

- The standard a financial professional is held to says a lot about their motivations. Professionals held to fiduciary standards of liability put *your* interests ahead of their own. Their success is tied to your success, and they are motivated not to sell you financial products, but help you create a lasting and successful retirement plan.
- A financial professional should focus on your goals, your risk tolerance, and your needs before recommending any specific financial products. Risk tolerance, need for liquidity, and other personal needs, goals, and circumstances should all be taken into consideration.
- Referrals can be a valuable and effective way to find a financial professional to work with. Your family and friends know you, and they can be trusted sources of information. That being said, you still need to do some research on anyone you plan to meet with. Check their references, read their resume, and learn about how they do business. Online resources can be a helpful tool in this process, including the National Association of Personal Financial Professionals, and the Financial Planning Association.
- Find out how often they meet with clients to update their plans, ask if you can see a sample plan, and learn about how they view money and investing. You want to work with someone you "click" with and who understands your viewpoint on money and investing.
- Not all investment firms and financial professionals are created equal. Working with an independent professional will give you more options that are customizable to your life.

# GLOSSARY*

**ANNUAL RESET** *(ANNUAL RATCHET, CLIQUET)* – Crediting methods measuring index movement over a one year period. Positive interest is calculated and credited at the end of each contract year and cannot be lost if the index subsequently declines. Say that the index increased from 100 to 110 in one year and the indexed annuity had an 80 percent participation rate. The insurance company would take the 10 percent gross index gain for the year (110-100/100), apply the participation rate (10 percent index gain x 80 percent rate) and credit 8 percent interest to the annuity. But, what if in the following year the index declined back to 100? The individual would keep the 8 percent interest earned and simply receive zero interest for the down year. An annual reset structure

* *"Glossary of Terms." FixedAnnuityFacts.com. NAFA, the National Association for Fixed Annuities, n.d. 12 Nov. 2013*

preserves credited gains and treats negative index periods as years with zero growth.

**ANNUITANT** – The person, usually the annuity owner, whose life expectancy is used to calculate the income payment amount on the annuity.

**ANNUITY** – An annuity is a contract issued by an insurance company that often serves as a type of savings plan used by individuals looking for long term growth and protection of assets that will likely be needed within retirement.

**AVERAGING** – Index values may either be measured from a start point to an end point (point-to-point) or values between the start point and end point may be averaged to determine an ending value. Index values may be averaged over the days, weeks, months or quarters of the period.

**BENEFICIARY** – A beneficiary is the person designated to receive payments due upon the death of the annuity owner or the annuitant themselves.

**BONUS RATE** – A bonus rate is the "extra" or "additional" interest paid during the first year (the initial guarantee period), typically used as an added incentive to get consumers to select their annuity policy over another.

**CALL OPTION** *(ALSO SEE PUT OPTION)* – Gives the holder the right to buy an underlying security or index at a specified price on or before a given date.

**CAP** – The maximum interest rate that will be credited to the annuity for the year or period. The cap usually refers to the maximum interest credited after applying the participation rate or yield spread. If the index methodology showed a 20 percent increase, the participation rate was 60 percent and the maximum interest cap was 10 percent, the contract would credit 10 percent interest. A few annuities use a maximum gain cap instead of a maximum interest cap with the participation rate or yield spread applied to the lesser of the gain or the cap. If the index methodology showed a 20 percent increase, the participation rate was 60 percent and the maximum gain cap was 10 percent, the contract would credit 6 percent interest.

**COMPOUND INTEREST** – Interest is earned on both the original principal and on previously earned interest. It is more favorable than simple interest. Suppose that your original principal was $1 and your interest rate was 10 percent for five years. With simple interest, your value is ($1 + $0.10 interest each year) = $1.50. With compound interest, your value is ($1 x 1.10 x 1.10 x 1.10 x 1.10 x 1.10) = $1.61. The advantage of compound interest over simple interest becomes greater as each subsequent period passes.

**CREDITING METHOD** *(ALSO SEE METHODOLOGY)* – The formula(s) used to determine the excess interest that is credited above the minimum interest guarantee.

**DEATH BENEFITS** – The payment the annuity owner's estate or beneficiaries will receive if he or she dies before the annuity matures. On most annuities, this is equal to the current account value. Some annuities offer an enhanced value at death via an optional rider that has a monthly or annual fee associated with it.

**EXCESS INTEREST** – Interest credited to the annuity contract above the minimum guaranteed interest rate. In an indexed annuity the excess interest is determined by applying a stated crediting method to a specific index or indices.

**FIXED ANNUITY** – A contract issued by an insurance company guaranteeing a minimum interest rate with the crediting of excess interest determined by the performance of the insurer's general account. Index annuities are fixed annuities.

**FIXED DEFERRED ANNUITY** – With fixed annuities, an insurance company offers a guaranteed interest rate plus safety of your principal and earnings ((subject to the claims-paying ability of the insurance company). Your interest rate will be reset periodically, based on economic and other factors, but is guaranteed to never fall below a certain rate.

**FREE WITHDRAWALS** – Withdrawals that are free of surrender charges.

**INDEX** – The underlying external benchmark upon which the crediting of excess interest is based, also a measure of the prices of a group of securities.

**IRA** *(INDIVIDUAL RETIREMENT ACCOUNT)* – An IRA is a tax-advantaged personal savings plan that lets an individual set aside money for retirement. All or part of the participant's contributions may be tax deductible, depending on the type of IRA chosen and the participant's personal financial circumstances. Distributions from many employer-sponsored retirement plans may be eligible to be rolled into an IRA to continue tax-deferred growth until the funds are needed. An annuity can be used as an IRA; that is, IRA funds can be used to purchase an annuity.

**IRA ROLLOVER** – IRA rollover is the phrase used when an individual who has a balance in an employer-sponsored retirement plan transfers that balance into an IRA. Such an exchange, when properly handled, is a tax-advantaged transaction.

**LIQUIDITY** – The ease with which an asset is convertible to cash. An asset with high liquidity provides flexibility, in that the owner can easily convert it to cash at any time, but it also tends to decrease profitability.

**MARKET RISK** – The risk of the market value of an asset fluctuating up or down over time. In a fixed or fixed indexed annuity, the original principal and credited interest are not subject to market risk. Even if the index declines, the annuity owner would receive no less than their original principal back if they decided to cash in the policy at the end of the surrender period. Unlike a security, indexed annuities guarantee the original premium and the premium is backed by, and is as safe as, the insurance company that issued it (subject to the claims-paying ability of the insurance company).

**METHODOLOGY** *(ALSO SEE CREDITING METHOD)* – The way that interest crediting is calculated. On fixed indexed annuities, there are a variety of different methods used to determine how index movement becomes interest credited.

**MINIMUM GUARANTEED RETURN** *(MINIMUM INTEREST RATE)* – Fixed indexed annuities typically provide a minimum guaranteed return over the life of the contract. At the time that the owner chooses to terminate the contract, the cash surrender value is compared to a second value calculated using the minimum guaranteed return and the higher of the two values is paid to the annuity owner.

**OPTION** – A contract which conveys to its holder the right, but not the obligation, to buy or sell something at a specified price on or before a given date. After this given date the option ceases to exist. Insurers typically buy options to provide for the excess interest potential. Options may be American style whereby they may be exercised at any time prior to the given date, or they may have to be exercised only during a specified window. Options that may only be exercised during a specified period are European-style options.

**OPTION RISK** – Most insurers create the potential for excess interest in an indexed annuity by buying options. Say that you could buy a share of stock for $50. If you bought the stock and it rose to $60 you could sell it and net a $10 profit. But, if the stock price fell to $40 you'd have a $10 loss. Instead of buying the actual stock, we could buy an option that gave us the right to buy the stock for $50 at any time over the next year. The cost of the option is $2. If the stock price rose to $60 we would exercise our option, buy the stock at $50 and make $10 (less the $2 cost of the option). If the price of the stock fell to $40, $30 or $10, we wouldn't use the option and it would expire. The loss is limited to $2—the cost of the option.

**PARTICIPATION RATE** – The percentage of positive index movement credited to the annuity. If the index methodology determined that the index increased 10 percent and the indexed annuity participated in 60 percent of the increase, it would be said that the contract has a 60 percent participation rate. Participation rates may also be expressed as asset fees or yield spreads.

**POINT-TO-POINT** – A crediting method measuring index movement from an absolute initial point to the absolute end point for a period. An index had a period starting value of 100 and a period ending value of 120. A point-to-point method would record a positive index movement of 20 [120-100] or a 20 percent positive movement [(120-100)/100]. Point-to-point usually refers to annual periods; however the phrase is also used instead of term end point to refer to multiple year periods.

**PREMIUM BONUS** – A premium bonus is additional money that is credited to the accumulation account of an annuity policy under certain conditions.

**PUT OPTION** *(ALSO SEE CALL OPTION)* – Gives the holder the right to sell an underlying security or index at a specified price on or before a given date.

**QUALIFIED ANNUITIES** *(QUALIFIED MONEY)* – Qualified annuities are annuities purchased for funding an IRA, 403(b) tax-deferred annuity or other type of retirement arrangements. An IRA or qualified retirement plan provides the tax deferral. An annuity contract should be used to fund an IRA or qualified retirement plan to benefit from an annuity's features other than tax deferral, including the safety features, lifetime income payout option and death benefit protection.

**REQUIRED MINIMUM DISTRIBUTION** *(RMD)* – The amount of money that Traditional, SEP and SIMPLE IRA owners and qualified plan participants must begin distributing from their retirement accounts by April 1 following the year they reach age 70.5. RMD amounts must then be distributed each subsequent year.

**RETURN FLOOR** – Another way of saying minimum guaranteed return.

**ROTH IRA** – Like other IRA accounts, the Roth IRA is simply a holding account that manages your stocks, bonds, annuities, mutual funds and CD's. However, future withdrawals (including earnings and interest) are typically tax-advantaged once the account has been open for five years and the account holder is age 59.5.

**RULE OF 72** – Tells you approximately how many years it takes a sum to double at a given rate. It's handy to be able to figure out, without using a calculator, that when you're earning a 6 percent return, for example, by dividing 6 percent into 72, you'll find that it takes 12 years for money to double. Conversely, if you know it took a sum twelve years to double you could divide 12 into 72 to determine the annual return (6 percent).

**SIMPLE INTEREST** *(ALSO SEE COMPOUND INTEREST)* – Interest is only earned on the principal balance.

**SPLIT ANNUITY** – A split annuity is the term given to an effective strategy that utilizes two or more different annuity products—one designed to generate monthly income and the other to restore the original starting principal over a set period of time.

**STANDARD & POOR'S 500** *(S&P 500)* – The most widely used external index by fixed indexed annuities. Its objective is to be a benchmark to measure and report overall U.S. stock market performance. It includes a representative sample of 500 common stocks from companies trading on the New York Stock Exchange, American Stock Exchange, and NASDAQ National Market System. The index represents the price or market value of the underlying stocks and does not include the value of reinvested dividends of the underlying stocks.

**STOCK MARKET INDEX** – A report created from a type of statistical measurement that shows up or down changes in a specific financial market, usually expressed as points and as a percentage, in a number of related markets, or in an economy as a whole (i.e. S&P 500 or New York Stock Exchange).

**SURRENDER CHARGE** – A charge imposed for withdrawing funds or terminating an annuity contract prematurely. There is no industry standard for surrender charges, that is, each annuity product has its own unique surrender charge schedule. The charge is usually expressed as a percentage of the amount withdrawn prematurely from the contract. The percentage tends to decline over time, ultimately becoming zero.

**TRADITIONAL IRA** – See <u>IRA (Individual Retirement Account)</u>

**TERM END POINT** – Crediting methods measuring index movements over a greater timeframe than a year or two. The opposite of an annual reset method. Also referred to as a term point-to-point method. Say that the index value was at 100 on the first day of the period. If the calculated index value was at 150 at the end of the period the positive index movement would be 50 percent (150-100/100). The company would credit a percentage of this movement as excess interest. Index movement is calculated and interest credited at the end of the term and interim movements during the period are ignored.

**TERM HIGH POINT** *(HIGH WATER MARK)* – A type of term end point structure that uses the highest anniversary index level as the end point. Say that the index value was at 100 on the first day of the period, reached a value of 160 at the end of a contract year during the period, and ended the period at 150. A term high point method would use the 160 value—the highest contract anniversary point reached during the period, as the end point and the gross index gain would be 60 percent (160-100/100). The company would then apply a participation rate to the gain.

**TERM YIELD SPREAD** – A type of term end point structure which calculates the total index gain for a period, computes the annual compound rate of return deducts a yield spread from the annual rate of return and then recalculates the total index gain for the period based on the net annual rate. Say that an index increased from 100 to 200 by the end of a nine year period. This is the equivalent of an 8 percent compound annual interest rate. If the annuity had a 2 percent term yield spread this would be deducted from the annual interest rate (8 percent-2 percent) and the net rate would be credited to the contract (6 percent) for each of the nine years. Total index gain may also be computed by using the highest anniversary index level as the end point.

**VARIABLE ANNUITY** – A contract issued by an insurance company offering separate accounts invested in a wide variety of stocks and/or bonds. The investment risk is borne by the annuity owner. Variable annuities are considered securities and require appropriate securities registration.

**1035 EXCHANGE** – The 1035 exchange refers to the section of tax code that allows annuity owners the flexibility to exchange one annuity for another without incurring any immediate tax liabilities. This action is most often utilized when an annuity holder decides they want to upgrade an annuity to a more favorable one, but they do not want to activate unnecessary tax liabilities that would typically be encountered when surrendering an existing annuity contract.

**401(K) ROLLOVER** – See IRA Rollover

80633605R00132

Made in the USA
Lexington, KY
04 February 2018